MEATLESS MEALS FOR WORKING PEOPLE

Quick and Easy Vegetarian Recipes

By Debra Wasserman
& Charles Stahler

Baltimore, Maryland
Fourth Edition, 2004

The VRg. **VEGETARIAN** *Resource Group*

Fantastic Foods® is a sponsor of
Meatless Meals for Working People

FANTASTIC
ALWAYS NATURAL ®

fantasticfoods.com

Acknowledgements

Special thanks to Reed Mangels, PhD, RD, for doing the nutritional analysis for all the recipes and contributing her expertise to this book including the weekly low-cost menus. Thank you also to the following individuals who provided information: Jeanne Bartas, Ruth Blackburn, MS, RD, Sarah Blum, Davida Breier, Heather Gorn, Marie Henein, Suzanne Havala Hobbs, DrPH, RD, Barbara Lovitts, PhD., Jeannie McStay, Stephanie Reph, Brad Scott, Annabelle Simpson, Marna Golub-Smith, Ellen Tattenbaum, Linda Tyler, and Mike Vogel. And finally, thank you to John Peters for doing the wonderful illustrations and David Herring for proofreading updated parts of this edition.

Please note: The contents of *Meatless Meals for Working People* are not intended to provide medical advice. Medical advice should be obtained from a qualified health professional.

© Copyright 2004, by Debra Wasserman and Charles Stahler.
Published by The Vegetarian Resource Group
PO Box 1463, Baltimore, MD 21203.

Library of Congress Cataloging-in-Publication Data

Wasserman, Debra.
  Meatless meals for working people : quick and easy vegetarian recipes / Debra Wasserman & Charles Stahler. -- 4th ed.
    p. cm.
  Includes index.
  ISBN 0-931411-29-7
  1. Vegetarian cookery. 2. Quick and easy cookery. I. Stahler, Charles. II. Title.
  TX837.W32 2004
  641.5'636—dc22

                                                                2004018614

Printed in the United States of America

10 9 8 7 6 5 4 3 2

Table of Contents

Salads and Dressings

Soups

Lunch Ideas

Side Dishes

Vegetarianism in a Nutshell

Vegetarianism is the abstinence from meat, fish, and fowl. Among the many reasons for being a vegetarian are compassion for animals, aesthetic considerations, and ecological, economic, spiritual, and health reasons. The American Dietetic Association has affirmed that a vegetarian diet can meet all known nutrient needs. Like every diet, the key to a healthy vegetarian diet is simple. Eat a variety of foods, eat a lot of greens, and have high-fat, high-salt, empty-calorie foods as only a small part of your diet. For the growing number of vegetarians who are following a vegan life-style and abstain from all animal products, including milk, cheese, eggs, and honey, this also can be done easily, but you may want to talk to others who have been practicing this diet.

Fresh is Best, But...

Using frozen, canned, and prepackaged foods greatly decreases food preparation time whether you are on a vegetarian diet or a non-vegetarian diet. Beware, however, that many prepackaged foods are high in sodium and may have animal shortening in them.

FROZEN FOODS

Frozen foods can be stored easily, and quickly popped into the oven while you're changing your clothes after work. Frozen vegetables such as green beans, corn, and spinach can be cooked in a short time and eaten alone or combined with other ingredients. Be careful not to overcook the vegetables or use too much water when cooking them. Several frozen pasta and vegetable mixes can be found in supermarkets, including vegetarian entrées manufactured by natural foods companies, which can be served for lunch or dinner.

CANNED AND PREPACKAGED VEGETARIAN FOODS

Though often more expensive than preparing from scratch, there are numerous canned and prepackaged foods you can find in most supermarkets. These items can quickly be used to prepare a meal or simply have a snack.

DAIRY CASE

Your dairy case is packed full of vegetarian ingredients and fast meal possibilities. Corn and wheat tortillas can easily be heated up and stuffed with leftover bean, grain, and/or vegetable mixtures.

Suggested Vegetarian Meals

Listed below are quick dishes and food items that you probably know how to cook already and can be made from common foods found in supermarkets. For a main meal, you may have one large central dish, a sandwich with or without soup, or several side dishes. Remember, the key to any healthy diet is variety.

BREAKFAST ITEMS:
These can easily be served as part of a main meal. You can substitute 1 small mashed ripe banana for each egg when making batter for French toast or using pancake and waffle mixes.

Frozen Breakfast Foods
Amy's Organic Toaster Pops
Bagels
Biscuits
Meatless Breakfast Patties and Links
Van's Waffles (flax, soy, etc.)

Other Breakfast Foods
Applesauce
Breads (English muffins, cornbread, rye, etc.)
Dry Cereal (Grape-Nuts, Muesli, Puffed Kashi, etc.)
Hot Cereal (Cream of Rice and Cream of Wheat, Farina, grits, oatmeal, Wheatena, etc.)
Fresh Fruit
Fruit Butters (apple butter, etc.)
Granola
Health Valley Cereal Bars
Jams (fruit sweetened variety is best)
Soy Yogurt
Wheat Germ

SANDWICHES:
Nut Butter (peanut, cashew, almond, etc.) and Jam
Bagels and Hummus (chickpea spread)
Nut Butter and Sliced Fruit (banana, apple, pear)
Sloppy Joe Sauce and Vegetables
Baked Beans and Lettuce on Toast
Tofu Salad (mashed tofu, minced celery, grated
    carrot, sweet relish, soy mayonnaise)
Chickpea Salad (mashed chickpeas, grated carrot,
    minced celery, dill weed, mayonnaise)

<u>Breads</u>
Bagels
English Muffins
French Bread
Hard Rolls
Italian Bread
Kaiser Rolls
Pita Bread
Pumpernickle Bread
Raisin Bread
Rye Bread
Tortillas
Whole Wheat Bread

MAIN MEALS (lunch or dinner):
<u>Frozen Main Dishes</u>
The following list is by no means complete, rather just a start.

Amy's Kitchen
    Asian Noodle Stir-Fry
    Organic Beans and Rice Burrito
    Organic Black Bean Vegetable Burrito
    Organic Breakfast Burrito
    Roasted Vegetable Pizza

Boca Foods Company
>   Vegan Boca Burger

Gardenburger Inc.
>   Buffalo Chik'n Wings
>   Flame Grilled Chik'n
>   Meatless Breakfast Sausage
>   Meatless Meatloaf
>   Meatless Riblets
>   Meatless Sweet and Sour Pork

Gardenburger Inc. Gardenburgers
>   Black Bean
>   Flame Grilled
>   Garden Vegan
>   Homestyle Classic
>   Vegetable Medley

Morningstar Farms
>   Better'n Burgers
>   Chili Pot Pie
>   Ground Meatless Crumbles
>   Vegan Burger

Health is Wealth
>   Buffalo Wings
>   Chicken-Free Nuggets
>   Chicken-Free Patties

Nate's
>   Classic Flavor Meatless Meatballs
>   Zesty Italian Meatless Meatballs

ETHNIC FOODS FOR MAIN MEALS (LUNCH OR DINNER):

<u>Asian</u>
Canned Vegetables (water chestnuts, baby corn, etc.)
Coconut Milk
Mustards
Rice Noodles
Sauces and Marinades (be sure to watch out for non-vegetarian fats and broths)

<u>Jewish</u>
Borscht
Falafel Mix
Hummus
Kasha
Mandlen for Soup (soup nuts)
Matzo
Matzo Meal
Potato Pancakes
Soup Mixes
Tahini (sesame butter)
Tam Tam Crackers
Tea Biscuits

<u>Mexican</u>
Burrito and Taco Kits
Fajita Marinade
Green Chiles
Guava and Mango Paste
Salsa
Taco Sauces and Seasoning Mixes
Tortillas and Taco Shells
Vegetarian Refried Beans (without lard)

<u>Middle Eastern</u>
Falafel Mix
Hummus (canned)
Hummus Mix
Tahini Sauce

PASTA:
Most pasta sold in packages in supermarkets doesn't contain eggs, unless it is called "egg pasta." Please note that fresh pasta often contains eggs. Look for eggless brands including Barilla, De-Boles, Mueller's, and San Giorgio.

PASTA SAUCES:
Amy's Premium Organic Pasta Sauce
>Family Marinara
>Pomodoro Zucca
>Tomato Basil
>Wild Mushroom

Classico
>Fire-Roasted Tomato and Garlic
>Mushrooms and Ripe Olives
>Spicy Red Pepper
>Sweet Basil Marinara
>Tomato and Basil

Millina's Finest Fat Free
>Organic Garlic Pasta Sauce
>Organic Marinara and Zinfandel Pasta Sauce
>Organic Tomato and Basil Pasta Sauce
>Organic Tomato Mushroom Pasta Sauce

Muir Glen
>Chunky Tomato and Herb
>Garden Vegetable
>Garlic and Onion
>Garlic Roasted Garlic
>Italian Herb
>Portabello Mushroom
>Sundried Tomato
>Tomato Basil

Newman's Own
> Marinara
> Mushroom Marinara
> Tomato and Fresh Basil
> Tomato, Peppers, and Spices
> Tomato Roasted Garlic

Walnut Acres Certified Organic
> Garlic Garlic
> Marinara and Zinfandel
> Portabello Marinara
> Tomato and Basil

VEGETARIAN DRY MIXES TO MAKE MAIN MEALS:
Fantastic Foods
> Black Beans
> Falafel
> Hummus
> Nature's Burger
> Refried Beans
> Sloppy Joe Mix
> Tabouli
> Taco Filling
> Tofu Buger
> Vegetarian Chili

DAIRY CASE ITEMS:
Flour and Corn Tortillas
Fruit Salad in Jars
Guacamole
Juice
Rice Milk
Salsa
Soy Creamer
Soy Milk
Soy Yogurt

ITEMS FOUND IN PRODUCE SECTION BESIDES PRODUCE:
Chopped Garlic, Jalapeño Peppers, etc.
Meat Alternatives (Burgers, Deli Slices, Hot Dogs, Meatless
    Ground, Veggie Bacon, Veggie Sausage, etc.)
Polenta
Salad Dressings
Soy Cheese
Sun-Dried Tomatoes
Tempeh
Tofu

ITEMS FOUND IN THE DELI COUNTER SECTION:
Dilled Cucumbers
Hummus
Olives
Tabouli
Vegetable Salads

SIDE DISHES:
Amy's Organic Chili
Bush's Vegetarian Baked Beans
Campbell's Vegetarian Beans in Tomato Sauce
Hanover Vegetarian Baked Beans
Heinz Vegetarian Beans in Tomato Sauce
Old El Paso Vegetarian Refried Beans
Walnut Acres Maple and Onion Baked Beans

Canned Beans
Black Beans
Black Eye Peas
Cannellini (white kidney beans)
Fava Beans
Garbanzo Beans (chickpeas)
Northern Beans
Pinto Beans
Red Kidney Beans

Dried Beans (Hint: Use a pressure cooker for quick
       and easy cooking of dried beans.)
Baby Lima Beans
Black Beans
Black Eye Peas
Garbanzo Beans (chickpeas)
Great Northern Beans
Green Split Peas
Kidney Beans
Lentils
Lima Beans
Mixed Beans for Soups
Navy Beans
Northern Beans
Pinto Beans
Roman Beans
Yellow Split Peas

Frozen Side Dishes
Empire Kosher Potato Pancakes
French Fries (make sure there is no animal flavor or fat)
Gabila's Potato Knishes
Hashbrowns (make sure there is no animal flavor or fat)
Onion Rings (make sure there is no animal flavor, animal fat, or
       eggs)
Tater Tots (make sure there is no animal flavor or fat)
Vegetable and Pasta Combinations

Grains
Arrowhead Mills
       Amaranth
       Buckwheat Groats
       Bulgur Wheat
       Quinoa
       Whole Millet

Casbah
> Couscous
> Couscous, Lentil, Rice, or Spanish Pilaf
> Tabouli

Fantastic Foods
> Arborio Rice
> Basmati Rice
> Couscous and Organic Whole Wheat Couscous
> Four Grain Rice Pilaf
> Jasmine Rice
> Tabouli

Lundberg Family Farms
> Organic Arborio
> Organic California Brown Basmati
> Organic California Brown Jasmine
> Organic Short Grain Brown Rice
> Organic Sushi Rice
> Wild Rice Blend

Near East
> Couscous
> Lentil Pilaf
> Rice Pilaf
> Taboule Wheat Salad
> Wheat Pilaf

Old World
> Bulgur Wheat

Quaker
> Barley

Rice Select
> Jasmati, Kasmati, Risotto, Sushi, or Texmati Rice

Uncle Ben's
    Brown Rice

Wolff's
    Kasha

Instant Seasoned Rice
Mahatma One Step Dish
    Saffron Yellow Seasonings and Rice

Manischewitz
    Brown Rice Pilaf Mix
    Lentil Pilaf Mix
    Rice Pilaf Mix
    Spanish Pilaf Mix
    Wheat Pilaf Mix

Near East
    Long Grain and Wild Rice
    Spanish Rice Pilaf

Rice A Roni
    Original Long Grain and Wild Rice
    Spanish Rice

Rice Select
    Shiitake Mushroom Rice
    Smokey Cowboy Rice and Beans
    Sonoran Mexican Rice

Uncle Ben's
    Long Grain and Wild Rice Original Recipe

Canned Vegetables
Artichokes
Asparagus
Beets
Carrots
Collard Greens
Corn (regular and cream style)
Green Beans
Green Peas
Hearts of Palm
Hominy (grits)
Kale
Lima Beans
Mixed Vegetables
Mushrooms
Okra
Sauerkraut
Spinach
Succotash (lima beans and corn)
Sweet Peas
Sweet Potatoes
Tomatoes
Turnip Greens
Wax Beans
White Potatoes
Yams

Frozen Vegetables
Artichoke Hearts
Asparagus
Bell Peppers
Black Eye Peas
Broccoli
Brussels Sprouts
Carrots
Cauliflower

Collard Greens
Corn
Green Beans
Green Peas
Kale
Lima Beans
Mixed Vegetables
Mustard Greens
Okra
Onions
Peas and Carrots
Spinach
Squash
Succotash
Turnip Greens

SOUPS:
Amy's Organic Soups
   Low Fat Black Bean Vegetable
   Low Fat Lentil
   Low Fat Minestrone
   Low Fat No Chicken Noodle
   Low Fat Split Pea
   Low Fat Vegetable Barley

Bean Cuisine (dry seasoned mixes found either near canned soups or dry beans)
   Island Black Bean
   Lots of Lentil Soup
   Santa Fe Corn Chowder
   Thick as Fog Split Pea
   13 Bean Bouillabaisse
   Ultima Pasta e Fagioli
   White Bean Provencal

Dr. McDougall's (cups of soup/meals)
   Baked Ramen Noodle Soup
   Minestrone
   Pinto Beans and Rice
   Rice and Pasta Pilaf
   Split Pea with Barley Soup
   Tamale Pie
   Tortilla soup

Fantastic Foods (cups of soup/meals)
   Cha Cha Chili Big Cup
   Country Lentil Big Cup
   Couscous with Lentils Big Cup
   Five Bean Soup Big Cup
   Hot and Sour Big Soup
   Jumpin' Black Bean Big Cup
   Mandarin Broccoli Big Soup
   Miso with Tofu Big Soup
   Split Pea Big Cup
   Spring Vegetable Big Soup
   Vegetable Barley Big Cup
   Vegetable Chicken Free Ramen Noodle Big Cup
   Vegetable Miso Ramen Noodle Big Cup

Fantastic Soup and Dip Recipe Mix
   Garlic Herb
   Onion

Health Valley
   Organic Black Bean Soup
   Organic Lentil Soup
   Organic Potato Leek Soup
   Organic Split Pea Soup
   Organic Tomato Soup

Health Valley Fat-Free
   5 Bean Vegetable
   14 Garden Vegetable

Health Valley Fat-Free or Lowfat (cups of soup/meals)
   Cantonese Rice
   Chili
   Garden Split Pea
   Lentil with Couscous
   Pasta Italiano
   Shiitake Rice
   Spicy Black Bean with Couscous
   Zesty Black Bean with Rice

Healthy Choice
   Country Vegetable
   Garden Vegetable

Imagine Organic
   Creamy Broccoli Soup
   Creamy Butternut Squash Soup
   Creamy Portobello Mushroom Soup
   Creamy Potato Leek Soup
   Creamy Sweet Corn Soup
   Creamy Tomato Soup

Lipton Recipe Soup Mix Recipe Secrets (powder)
   Onion
   Onion-Mushroom
   Vegetable

Pacific Foods All Natural Soup
    Creamy Butternut Squash
    Organic Vegetable Broth

Progresso Soup
    Lentil

Walnut Acres Certified Organic
    Lentil Soup
    Split Pea soup
    Tuscan White Bean Soup
    Vine-Ripened Tomato Soup

Westbrae Natural
    Alabama Black Bean Gumbo
    Great Plains Savory Bean
    Louisiana Bean Stew
    Mediterranean Lentil
    Old World Split Pea
    Santa Fe Vegetable
    Spicy Southwest Vegetable

GRAVY AND SAUCES:
Annie's
    Smokey Maple BBQ Sauce

Hain Pure Foods
    Vegetarian Brown Gravy Mix
    Vegetarian Chicken Flavored Gravy Mix

Hunt's
    Manwich Sloppy Joe Sauce

Loma Linda Fat Free Gravy Quik
    Vegetarian Brown Gravy Mix
    Vegetarian Chicken Style Gravy Mix
    Vegetarian Country Style Gravy Mix
    Vegetarian Mushroom Gravy Mix
    Vegetarian Onion Gravy Mix

SNACK ITEMS:
Cookies
Corn Chips
Dips
Dried Fruits (raisins, dates, prunes, figs, etc.)
Fruit Leather
Granola Bars
Nuts
Popcorn
Potato Chips (watch for lard in ingredients)
Pretzels
Rice Cakes
Salsa
Seeds (sunflower, pumpkin, etc.)
Trail Mix

Crackers
Carr's Table Water Crackers
    Original
    With Cracked Pepper
    With Roasted Garlic and Herbs
    With Toasted Sesame Seeds

Carr's Whole Wheat Crackers

Devonsheer Melba Toast and Melba Rounds
    Garlic
    Plain
    Rye
    Sesame
    Vegetable
    Wheat

Frookie Snack Crackers
    Wheat and Onion
    Wheat and Rye

Hol Grain Crackers
    Brown Rice A Light Touch of Salt
    Brown Rice No Salt
    Brown Rice Onion and Garlic

Keebler Club Partners
    Original
    Reduced Fat
    Reduced Sodium

Keebler Toasteds
　　　Onion
　　　Rye
　　　Savory Crisps (multigrain and roasted garlic)
　　　Sesame
　　　Wheat

Keebler Townhouse Crackers
　　　Classic
　　　Reduced Fat

Keebler Zesta Saltine Crackers

Nabisco
　　　Harvest Crisps—5 Grain
　　　Harvest Crisps—Garden Vegetable
　　　Low Sodium Ritz Crackers
　　　Ritz Crackers
　　　Ritz Crackers with Whole Wheat
　　　Ritz Sticks
　　　Soup and Oyster Crackers
　　　Uneeda Biscuit
　　　Waverly

Nabisco Premium Saltine Crackers
　　　Fat Free
　　　Low Sodium
　　　Original
　　　Unsalted Tops
　　　With Multi-Grain

Nabisco Triscuit
> Deli Style Rye
> Garden Herb
> Low Sodium
> Original
> Reduced Fat
> Roasted Garlic
> Wheat N' Bran

Nabisco Wheat Thins
> Low Sodium
> Multi-Grain
> Original
> Reduced Fat

Ralston Saltines
> Original
> Unsalted Tops

Sunshine Krispy Original Saltine Crackers

Wasa
> Fiber Rye Crispbread
> Hearty Rye Crispbread
> Light Rye Crispbread
> Sourdough Rye Crispbread

DESSERTS:
Canned fruit
Apples
Applesauce
Berries
Cherries
Citrus Fruit
Cranberry Sauce
Peaches
Pears
Pineapple

Cookies
Barbara's Bakery
      Blueberry Fig Bars
      Traditional Fig Bars
      Wheat Free Fig Bars
      Whole Wheat Fig Bars

Frookie All Natural
      Frookwich Chocolate
      Frookwich Vanilla
      Funky Monkeys Chocolate

Kedem Tea Biscuits
      Chocolate
      Plain
      Vanilla

Keebler Grahams
      Chocolate
      Cinnamon Crisp
      Original

Nabisco
>Golden Oreo
>Grahams—Original
>Mini Oreo
>Teddy Grahams—Cinnamon

Newman's Own Organics
>Alphabet Cookies (wheat-free/dairy-free)
>Fig Newmans (wheat-free/dairy-free)
>Newman's Ginger O's
>Newman's-O's (wheat-free/dairy-free)

<u>Frozen Desserts</u>
Marie Callender's
>Apple, Cherry Crunch, Dutch Apple, and Razzleberry Pie

Pepperidge Farms
>Apple and Raspberry Turnovers

TAKE-OUT FOODS:
The quickest way to prepare a meal is to take out food. Stop at your local deli counter and pick up potato salad, health salads, hummus, salsa, and other goodies. Ethnic fast food places are also good sources for a quick bite. You can purchase Mexican bean tacos or burritos, vegetable lo mein, and/or stir-fried vegetables. Chinese and Thai restaurants are usually happy to prepare any dish without meat if you politely ask. Be sure to request that they do not use fish sauce. Italian pizza and eggplant subs are also terrific items. Some restaurants still fry their food in lard, so you may want to ask some questions before ordering a meal.

Eating Out

Eating out is getting easier and easier for both vegetarians and vegans. If you have a choice, try an ethnic restaurant. Besides Chinese, Mexican, and Italian, good vegetarian eateries (especially in cities) include Indian, Middle Eastern, Thai, Ethiopian, Japanese, and Vietnamese. And, of course, even quick service restaurant chains and truck stops now offer salad bars or other vegetarian choices. For a list of vegetarian restaurants throughout the United States visit http://vrg.org/restaurant/ index.htm

TRUCK STOPS AND SHOPPING CENTERS:
The following is a list of some of the vegetarian items we've found in these places.

Salad Bars
Grits
Oatmeal
Hash Browns (make sure they are not fried in lard and do not
  contain bacon)
Waffles and Pancakes
English Muffins, Bagels, etc.
Salads
Vegetarian Soups
French Fries or Onion Rings (make sure they are not fried in
  animal fat)
Lettuce, Tomato, and Vegetable Sandwiches
Coleslaw
Eggplant Subs
Bean Burritos
Veggie Burgers
Side Orders of Vegetables (make sure they do not contain ham)
Pretzels

BOARDWALKS, CARNIVALS, PARKS, AND BALL PARKS:
Even these havens of typical Americana have items for the vegetarian or vegan. (Also see information on ballparks at http://www.soyhappy.org/venue.htm)

Sorbet or Italian Ices
French Fries and Onion Rings (make sure they are not fried in
    lard)
Pizza (can be ordered without cheese and with extra vegetables)
Fresh Fruit Cups
Pretzels with Mustard
Fruit Shakes
Funnel Cakes or Fried Dough
Corn on the Cob
French Fried Vegetables
Vegetable Subs
Popcorn

VEGETARIAN FOOD ON AIRLINES:
Today, to save money, many airlines no longer offer meals on domestic flights. However, if your flight does offer a meal and you require a special meal for reasons of health, religion, or personal preference, most airlines will accommodate your needs if you let them know at least 24 hours before your flight departs. We would recommend that you describe your food requirements when making your reservation and then remind the airline again 24 hours before your departure time.

Special meals available may include vegetarian with dairy, vegetarian without dairy or eggs (vegan), diabetic, low-fat, etc. Be specific about what you are requesting. Beware that a low-fat meal probably contains an animal product. Also, quite often airlines forget your special meal request. Therefore, it's best to bring along your own food (especially on long flights).

Vegetarian and Vegan Menu Items at Restaurant and Quick Service Chains

Some people keep strictly kosher and will never eat in a non-kosher restaurant. Likewise, some vegetarians will never dine in a non-vegetarian establishment since they can never be sure that an item is 100 percent vegetarian or vegan. However, most vegetarians eat out, and each person decides where to draw his or her line. We encourage restaurants to try to meet the needs of vegetarians and for vegetarians to do the best they can. Please realize that life isn't perfect, and mistakes can be made. If we want a better world, let's work together in a positive way so it will be easier for you to be vegetarian and for restaurants to offer vegetarian options.

PLEASE NOTE: We depend on company statements for product and ingredient information. It is impossible to be 100 percent sure about a statement, information can change, people have different views, and mistakes can be made. Please use your own best judgement about whether a product is suitable for you. To be certain, do further research or confirmation on your own. If you want to be 100 percent sure, we suggest you do not eat items from these establishments. If you are like the majority of Americans, please do the best you can.

The contents of this book and our other publications, including web information, are not intended to provide personal medical advice. Medical advice should be obtained from a qualified health professional.

For political reasons, some people choose not to support quick service chains. Others believe that since so many people, especially young people, patronize these establishments, the best strategy is to encourage that vegetarian items be offered. For example, People for the Ethical Treatment of Animals (PETA) has heavily promoted Burger King's veggie burger. Some vegetarians are very concerned about "micro-ingredients" which may make an item non-vegetarian (e.g. white sugar processed with bone char). At the same time, some vegan and animal rights groups and activists feel this approach is counterproductive, because it may discourage businesses from promoting foods as vegetarian, is not practical for the majority of Americans, and keeps people from being vegetarian and vegan. They believe that if everyone was vegetarian (no meat, fish, and fowl) or vegan (vegetarians who also abstain from dairy or eggs), then micro-ingredients would no longer be used. This perspective is not meant to be an excuse to purposely use non-vegetarian ingredients but for consumers and food businesses to do the best they can and evolve to a higher ideal. While companies should respect vegetarians' needs, vegetarians should under-stand the difficult challenges of running restaurants.

Numerous food companies have worked to have restaurants carry vegetarian items on their menus. For example, Veggie-Land™ said their burger has been offered at Houlihan's, Ground Round, Chili's, and even in Universal City. Morningstar Farms Burgers have been sold at Burger King, and McDonald's has been testing Yves (Hain) burgers in California. Yet even if vege-tarian options are not listed, it is possible to order menu items without certain ingredients; you just need to ask. For instance, tacos and pizzas can be ordered without cheese at some restaurant chains that serve these foods. Taco Bell even has a brochure, "Want Lower-Fat Choices? Try it Fresco Style." They state, "Fresco Style reduces fat by 25% for most menu items compared to the original menu item." Fresco Style simply means substituting Fiesta Salsa for cheese and sauce in any of your Taco Bell favorites. Furthermore, many restaurants would be happy to make specially requested items for their guests.

PLEASE NOTE: Most restaurant chains are unsure whether the enzymes used in their cheeses are microbial- or animal-derived. Some chains said that typically the enzyme used is microbial, but they could not guarantee this because suppliers may use whatever enzyme is available. At this time, if a restaurant or food company in the United States calls their lacto-ovo food vegetarian, it may not guarantee that the cheese is made with vegetable rennet. If you are concerned about this, you should avoid items with cheese.

The vegetarian or vegan can be wary about "hidden" ingredients (such as gelatin in guacamole or a danish) or objectionable preparation methods (such as frying hash browns in the same oil used to fry meat or seafood products). It is always best to ask at a particular restaurant. If the given answer is not satisfactory, try contacting the corporate headquarters in a pleasant way. Ask the manager at the particular restaurant for the phone number, or try the company's website. Likewise, if you are happy with a vegetarian or vegan meal at a restaurant chain or have suggestions on how a restaurant menu can be made more veggie-friendly, please let the manager or corporate head-quarters know! Without a demand for vegetarian or vegan options, restaurants remove these offerings from their menus.

Suppliers and ingredients are ever-changing. When you are purchasing foods, an exact guarantee of the ingredients is probably not possible. In many cases companies label their items as vegetarian or vegan when there could be a few "maybe" ingredients, such as mono- and diglycerides. Everyone draws the line as to what he or she will eat in a different place. If you want to be safer, we suggest you do more research on your own.

Many restaurant websites now list ingredients, with some being more complete than others. When you talk to a customer service representative or a quality assurance manager in a positive way about the sources of an ingredient, such as natural flavors or mono- and diglycerides, you are educating people about the concerns of vegetarians and vegans. You are also helping the next person who inquires about that ingredient, too. We have an interesting situation where a chain may offer an item from a company that manufactures products that vegetarians will eat at home. However, the chain may state they can not guarantee that any food they offer is vegetarian. This may be to protect the chain. Also, problems arise because some vegetarians will use a particular food while others won't, restaurants may not always use a separate cooking surface for meat and vegetarian foods, it is very easy to make a mistake in food service, etc. This approach of stating that the establishment has nothing vegetarian appears to warn the concerned vegetarian and protect the business, but it doesn't inform the vegetarian who wishes to eat out. We will be interested to see how restaurants and the vegetarian movement solve this problem.

Restaurants seem to want to further research the sources of their ingredients so as to serve better their vegetarian and vegan guests. Although these requests do not guarantee that restaurant chains will make changes in their ingredients or menus, they represent a first step toward this result. Some chains are testing vegetarian options in a few of their restaurants. If you are in any restaurant where a vegetarian or vegan option is being offered, showing your support and purchasing the food item is a way to keep vegetarian and vegan options on the menus or to put them there in the first place. Perhaps one day there will be many all-vegetarian or all-vegan national restaurant chains.

Please use this guide to restaurant chains only as a starting point, not as definite answers. Menus and ingredients do change, sometimes suddenly and without well-publicized notification. If you see information which you believe is incorrect, please let us know. Visit <www.vrg.org> for updates.

Definitions:

VEGETARIAN AND VEGAN
Vegetarian items do not contain meat, fish, or fowl. Vegan foods, in addition to being vegetarian, are free of all animal ingredients, including dairy products and eggs.

GELATIN
Gelatin can be made from cows, pigs, fish, and other animals. It is animal protein used especially for its thickening and gelling properties. It is often in candies. Kosher gelatin can be made with fish and/or beef. (Viewpoint, Vol 30, #4)

MONO- AND DIGLYCERIDES
Monoglycerides and diglycerides are common food additives used to blend certain ingredients together, such as oil and water, which would not otherwise blend well. They are often found in bakery products, beverages, ice cream, chewing gum, shortening, whipped toppings, margarine, and confections. The commercial source may be either animal (cow- or hog-derived) or vegetable, and they may be synthetically made as well. Archer Daniels Midland Co., a large manufacturer of monoglycerides, reported that they use soybean oil.

NATURAL FLAVORS
The definition of natural flavorings and flavors from 21CFR101.22 (the Code of Federal Regulations) is as follows:

"The term natural flavor or natural flavoring means the essential oil, oleoresin, essence or extractive, protein hydrolysate, distillate, or any product of roasting, heating or enzymolysis, which contains the flavoring constituents derived from a spice, fruit or fruit juice, vegetable or vegetable juice, edible yeast, herb, bark, bud, root, leaf or similar plant material, meat, seafood, poultry, eggs, dairy products, or fermentation products thereof, whose significant function in food is flavoring rather than nutritional."

In other words, natural flavors can be pretty much anything approved for use in food. It's nearly impossible to tell what is in natural flavors unless the company has specified it on the label. A few of the vegetarian- and vegan-oriented companies are doing this now, but the overwhelming majority of food manufacturers do not.

Why do companies "hide" ingredients under "natural flavors?" It's considered a way of preserving the product's identity and uniqueness. This is similar to thinking behind a "secret recipe." Company executives worry that someone would be able to duplicate their product if they publish what their products' flavorings were.

So, what is a vegetarian to do? Call the company. Ask them what's in the flavorings. They may not be able to tell you, but the more they hear this question, the more likely they are to become concerned about putting a clarifying statement on their labels. It does work in some cases (such as when a significant number of people wrote to the USDA about standardizing the qualities necessary for a product to be classified as organic), although it may take awhile. We have already had several large food companies contact us about their natural flavors and how to word their labels if they use only vegetarian or vegan flavorings. They called because it had come to their attention that this was a concern for vegetarians and vegans.

RENNET

Typically, cheese is made by coagulating cow or goat's milk with rennet or rennin (an enzyme). Traditionally, rennet was from a calf's stomach. There are also cheeses, which are made with vegetable or microbial enzymes (rennet). In most non-vegetarian restaurant in the United States, it's unlikely restaurant staff will know what kind of cheese is being used.

For information about over 200 food ingredients, send $6 to:
Guide to Food Ingredients, The Vegetarian Resource Group,
P.O. Box 1463, Baltimore, MD 21203
Or order online at: <www.vrg.org/catalog/order.htm>

Please use this guide to restaurant chains only as a starting point, not as definite answers. Menus and ingredients do change, sometimes suddenly and without well-publicized notification. If you see information which you believe is incorrect, please let us know.

APPLEBEE'S: When contacted about vegetarian and vegan menu items, Applebee's responded with the following statement:

"We have made a recent decision to discontinue our vegetarian menu items in most of our restaurants... Unfortunately, the sales of these items were not sufficient enough for us to continue to offer them on our menu.

Your server, or the manager on duty at any of our restaurants, will be happy to assist you in selecting an entrée that meets your taste and dietary needs! The good news is that any of the following items can be made 'meatless.' The items listed, which can be made 'meatless' are: Chicken & Broccoli Pasta Alfredo, Nachos Nuevos, Chicken Fajita Roll-Up, Sizzling Stir-Fry, and Fajitas."

No further ingredient information was received about these items. Please note that the Chicken Quesadilla contains bacon pieces, so omitting the chicken would not create a meatless dish.

ARBY'S: Over the phone, Arby's indicated that basically they only had meat-based items and vegetarians would not find many options on their menu.

According to the Arby's website, their Garden Salad contains lettuce, tomatoes, broccoli, cucumbers, and shredded carrots. The Side Salad contains lettuce, tomatoes, and shredded carrots.

Their Deluxe Baked Potato consists of baked potato, butter or margarine/butter blend, sour cream, shredded cheddar cheese, bacon bits, and chives. Note that their sour cream contains gelatin.

The Homestyle Fries contain potatoes, partially hydrogenated vegetable shortening (soybean oil and/or canola oil), modified food starch, rice flour, dextrin, salt, leavening (disodium dihydrogen pyrophosphate, sodium bicarbonate), dextrose, and xanthan gum. The Potato Cakes contain potatoes, partially hydrogenated vegetable shortening (soybean oil and/or canola oil), salt, corn flour, dehydrated potato flakes, natural flavoring (unspecified origin), disodium dihydrogen pyrophosphate (to promote color retention), and dextrose.

Their Sourdough Bread contains enriched wheat flour, water, yeast, high fructose corn syrup, rye flour, salt, soybean oil, acetic acid, vinegar, monoglycerides (unspecified origin), calcium sulfate, xanthan gum, enzyme active soy flour, guar gum, sodium stearoyl lactylate, datem, sunflower oil, cornstarch, and calcium propionate.

Their Biscuits, among other ingredients, contain dairy, egg, and natural flavors (source not indicated). Their Croissants contain patent flour, high protein flour, butter, milk, sugar, yeast, and salt. The croutons, among other ingredients, contain milk and cheese with unspecified enzymes.

Their Marinara Dipping Sauce contains tomato purée (water and tomato paste), soybean oil, high fructose corn syrup, dry onion, garlic, salt, spices, citric acid, and xanthan gum.

Arby's Apple Turnover consists of unbleached wheat flour, apples, water, sugar, high fructose corn syrup, partially hydrogenated vegetable shortening (soybean oil colored with beta carotene), corn syrup, raisins, modified food starch, salt, dextrin, distilled monoglycerides (from hydrogenated soybean oil), soy lecithin, and cinnamon.

AU BON PAIN: We did not receive our survey back from Au Bon Pain. On their website, they indicated as vegetarian: Mediterranean Wrap, Roma Tomato and Mozzarella Ficelle, French Moroccan Tomato Lentil Soup, Curried Rice and Lentil Soup, Corn and Green Chili Bisque, Vegetarian Lentil Soup, Old Fashioned Tomato Soup, Garden Vegetable Soup, Harvest Pumpkin Soup, Vegetarian Chili, and Vegetarian Minestrone.

Their plain bagel contains unbleached flour (wheat flour, malted barley flour), water, natural sourdough starter (wheat, flour, water), bagel base (sugar, salt, malted barley flour, and 2 percent or less of the following: molasses, DATEM, vegetable mono-diglycerides, enzymes, ammonium chloride, ascorbic acid, L-cysteine, potassium iodate, azodicarbonamide), brown sugar, and yeast. Check their website for ingredient listings.

Note that sources of enzymes are not listed with the ingredients as of this writing.

AUNTIE ANNE'S: Auntie Anne's stated that all of their pretzels and beverages are vegetarian and that their dips are vegetarian with the exception of Marinara Sauce and Cheese Sauce. They said that their pretzels do not contain ingredients from animal sources, except the Sour Cream and Onion Pretzel and the Parmesan Herb Pretzel. They dip their pretzels in real butter after they come out of the oven, but you can request "no butter" at time of order. Enzymes in cheeses are unknown.

BAJA FRESH: This company chose not to participate in our survey at this time. However, on their website, Baja Fresh indicates that they do not use lard and that these items are vegetarian: Grilled Vegetarian Burrito, Vegetarian Bare Burrito (served in a bowl instead of a tortilla), Tostada, Grilled Veggie Taco, Side Salad, Enchiladas, Enchiladas Verdes, Quesadilla, and Mini Quesa-Dita. Detailed ingredients are not given.

Baja Fresh says to contact them directly for specific questions.

BASKIN-ROBBINS: Previously, we received detailed answers from Baskin Robbins. This time, Customer Service said they are no longer releasing ingredient information from their supplier and that the supplier considers ingredient information proprietary. They stated that their Daiquiri Ice and Peach Keen were dairy-free, but they could not comment on whether they contain gelatin. We were also told that they have more than 1,000 flavors and it is too time consuming to provide this information.

BENNIGAN'S: They said they were interested in participating in our survey because of the current interest in healthy foods. As of this writing, we have not yet received the response. According to their website, they offer a Boca Burger topped with American cheese, mustard, and pickles. A Boca Burger patty may be substituted for beef in any of their burgers.

BOJANGLES': The hash browns (Botato Rounds) and seasoned fries at Bojangles' are cooked in a mix of animal and vegetable oils. This oil has been "seeded" with the oil that was used to cook chicken to impart flavor.

Bojangles' states that their cob corn, Cajun pintos, and marinated coleslaw are vegan. The creamy coleslaw contains egg yolk. The seasoning for the green beans contains bacon flavoring and bacon fat.

Their macaroni and cheese is made with pasteurized American cheese. The mashed potatoes contain nonfat dry milk and natural flavors of an unspecified nature.

All of the biscuits at Bojangles' contain buttermilk. The breakfast biscuit can be ordered without the meat, egg, and/or cheese upon request. None of their baked goods are free of milk, eggs, honey, and their derivatives. The sweet potato pie contains eggs, dairy, and beef tallow.

BOSTON MARKET: Boston Market reports that the following menu items are vegan: cranberry walnut relish, white carver roll, and fruit salad.

The company listed the following menu items as vegetarian: chunky cinnamon applesauce, broccoli with red peppers, brownies with chocolate chips, butternut squash, cheesecake, cinnamon apples, coleslaw, all cookies, buttered corn, cornbread, cranberry walnut relish, creamed spinach, fruit salad, green beans, green bean casserole, hummingbird cake, macaroni and cheese, mashed potatoes, new potatoes, apple streusel pie, cherry streusel pie, pecan pie, pumpkin pie, potato salad, honey wheat roll, white carver roll, steamed vegetables, sweet potatoes, and stuffing.

Boston Market does not fry its items. None of the vegetarian/vegan items are cooked in oil that has been used to cook meat or chicken, nor are these items cooked on the same surfaces that are used to cook meat or chicken. Any items that contain gelatin are not included on the list of Boston Market vegetarian and vegan items.

None of the baked goods contain animal shortening or lard. The Honey Wheat Roll and White Roll used on Boston Market sandwiches do not contain milk, eggs, or their derivatives. The Honey Wheat Roll contains honey. Any items that contain beef broth or chicken stock or other flavors that were animal-derived are not included on the vegetarian and vegan list. The items on their vegetarian list contain cheeses that use only vegetable/microbial-derived enzymes.

Boston Market would be happy to customize sandwiches, but all other items are standardized.

This restaurant chain issued the following disclaimers for the above information:

"This information applies to Boston Market in-restaurant items only. Boston Market catering and delivery menu items may differ.

"This information is based on standard product formulations and recipes. Variations can be expected due to slight differences in product assembly on a restaurant-by-restaurant basis and other factors. In order to ensure freshness of our products, Boston Market purchases many products and ingredients locally from numerous vendors, so that introduces factors of variability. Some of the listed products may not be available in all markets, and items that are in test markets or are regional in nature have not been listed. For further assistance, please call our Customer Care team at 800-365-7000.

"Data is current as of the time of publication of this guide, and new product introductions or product changes may cause deviations from the information listed. Neither Boston Market, nor its employees, assume responsibility for a particular sensitivity or allergy to any food provided in our restaurants."

BRUEGGER'S BAGEL BAKERY: According to their website, Bruegger's plain bagel contains enriched flour (wheat flour, malted barley flour, niacin, reduced iron, thiamin mononitrate, riboflavin, folic acid), water, malt syrup, salt, and yeast. Their Garden Veggie consists of a plain bagel, red onions, tomatoes, alfalfa sprouts, green bell peppers, cucumbers, and lettuce. Their hummus contains chickpeas (garbanzo beans), tahini (ground sesame), lemon juice, olive oil, parsley, garlic, and cumin.

BURGER KING: In 1997 we were told by Burger King that their French fries contained nothing "which would present a problem to (a vegetarian) diet. No whey, no dairy products, no beef fat, no flavoring from animals."

In 2002, however, Burger King Customer Relations stated that the fries are not considered to be vegetarian. We called BK's Media Relations department, and they stated that the fries do contain a small amount of a poultry-based amino acid used for flavoring. BK's Product Consistency Department informed us that the recipe for the French fry coating was reformulated in the spring of 2001.

On April 28, 2003, BK's Media Relations Department informed us that the poultry-derived amino acid is no longer part of the natural flavoring used on their French fries. In September 2003, Burger King told us to use the revised 10/1/2003 ingredient statement on their website. This states that the natural flavors in the French fries are from plant sources.

Burger King's Hash Brown Rounds also indicate that the natural flavors are from plant sources. Their French Fries are cooked in dedicated fryers; however, a common fryer is used to cook onion rings, French Toast Sticks, and Hash Brown Rounds. The BK French Toast Sticks contain natural flavors from animal and plant sources.

In 2002, Burger King announced they are offering the BK Veggie® burger on the national menu in the United States. The patty itself was produced by Morningstar Farms (a division of

Kellogg's) for Burger King.

On May 17, 2005, the Kellogg Company issued a press release announcing the launch of a new BK Veggie Burger in Burger King restaurants nationwide. The burger is made by Morningstar Farms, which is owned by the Kellogg Company.

The press release describes the burger as vegetarian. The Burger King website states that the burger contains egg whites and calcium caseinate, and the natural flavors are derived from non-animal sources. It also mentions that the veggie burgers are cooked separately from meat products. We called Burger King and have been told they are microwaving the burgers.

Alan Gravely, vice president of marketing, Kellogg's Frozen Foods, says "Consumers have told us that when they eat out they want the vegetarian options and great taste that Morningstar Farms gives them at home. We are excited that our relationship with Burger King Corporation will enable consumers to balance the convenience of dining out with their nutrition and diet priorities."

Customers who order the BK Veggie Burger will be able to customize as they do with regular Burger King burgers.

We would advise that you check back periodically with the Burger King's website to see if there have been reformulations of the burger or the buns. To ensure freshness of their buns and produce, Burger King restaurants states that they purchase these products locally from numerous vendors, thereby introducing a factor of variability, such as the need for optional ingredients. PLEASE NOTE that as of 2007, Burger King is still stating that "Burger King Corporation makes no claim that the BK Veggie® or any other of its products meet the requirements of a vegan or vegetarian diet."

CHI-CHI'S: According to Chi-Chi's: "Vegan foods contain no meat, fish, poultry, eggs, honey, dairy, or their derivatives (whey, casein).... Vegetarian foods contain no meat, fish or poultry."

The company lists the following menu items "vegan": Chi-Chi's Original Mild and Hot Garden Salsa, Ensalada del Casa (without cheese or Cotija Ranch Dressing), Guacamole, Vegetable Fajitas (without sour cream and cheese condiments), Refried Beans (without sour cream or cheese), Bean Burrito (without Enchilada Sauce and cheese), Bean Soft Taco (without cheese), and Fruit by the Foot®.

The following menu items are labeled "vegetarian": Fresh Vegetable Quesadilla, Chile Con Queso, Plain Ice Cream Sundae with choice of topping, Bean Soft Taco, Children's Pizza (no fries), and Children's Macaroni and Cheese (no fries).

Items that are fried in vegetable oil (such as Chips, Taco Shells, Chimichangas, etc.) are not considered vegetarian or vegan because meat products may also be fried in the same oil. Also note that the Mexican Rice, Cheese and Onion Enchiladas, all soups, and the Enchilada Sauce contain chicken stock. Rice at Chi-Chi's contains natural flavors derived from chicken and pork.

Chi-Chi's cannot guarantee that the type of enzyme used in their cheese is microbial. According to the company, microbial rennin is used most of the time, but their supplier cannot guarantee that it is always used.

The Vegetarian Quesadilla is cooked on the same surface that is used to cook other quesadillas (that contain meat products), but the only part that touches the surface is the tortilla wrap; none of the contents are cooked on the shared surface.

The Tortillas are free of milk, eggs, honey, and their derivatives.

Chi-Chi's is happy to prepare menu items differently upon request to accommodate a customer's special dietary needs.

CHUCK E. CHEESE'S: This company did not respond to our survey. They list a vegetarian pizza on their menu. The Chuck E. Cheese's website indicates that there is no animal rennet in their cheese. Readers have told us that there is no problem when asking their restaurants to make a pizza without cheese.

DENNY'S: Denny's did not respond to our survey as of this printing. According to their website, they carry a Boca Burger. For breakfast, the restaurant also offers an English muffin, bagel, Quaker oatmeal, Kellogg's dry cereal, Musselman's applesauce, banana, honeydew, cantaloupe, grapefruit, grapes, and fruit mix. Ingredients are not listed.

DOMINO'S: Domino's provided us a list of ingredients. They stated that "Ingredients not required to be listed by regulation may not be represented here. (Note: some products will not have all the ingredients as listed.)"

Their Hand Tossed Dough contains enriched wheat flour, water, vegetable oil, sugar, salt, yeast, vital wheat gluten, dough conditioners (ascorbic acid, L-cysteine, sodium stearoyl lactylate), whey, enzyme, cornmeal.

Among other ingredients, their Deep Dish Crust contains whey, imitation Parmesan cheese with casein, and natural flavor (source unspecified).

The ingredients listed for their Thin Crust are flour (wheat flour, malted barley flour), water, soybean oil, yeast, dextrose, leavening agents (sodium acid pyrophosphate, sodium bicarbonate, cornstarch, monocalcium phosphate), calcium propionate (preservative), and salt.

Their Pizza Sauce contains tomatoes, salt, sugar, water, garlic powder, black pepper, oregano, basil, and citric acid (less than 1 percent, may be added to control pH).

The Pizza Cheese contains mozzarella cheese (pasteurized milk, cultures, salt, enzymes of unspecified source), modified food starch, cellulose (added to prevent caking), non-fat milk, whey, protein concentrate, sodium citrate, flavors, and sodium propionate (added as a preservative).

The Breadsticks contain enriched wheat flour (niacin, iron, thiamine mononitrate, riboflavin, folic acid), water, vegetable oil (soybean), sugar, salt, yeast, vital wheat gluten, and less than 1 percent of: dough conditioners (ascorbic acid, L-cysteine, sodium stearoyl lactylate), whey, enzyme, and cornmeal.

The Marinara Sauce contains tomato purée (water, tomato paste) and less than 2 percent of salt, sugar, spices, ascorbic acid, erythorbic acid (preservative), garlic powder, xanthan gum, potassium sorbate (preservative), sodium benzoate (preservative), citric acid, natural flavor, and nisin (preservative, contains trace amount of denatured milk solids).

The Catalina French Dressing (packets) contains soybean oil, water, sugar, vinegar, tomato paste, salt, xanthan gum (less than 2%), dried onion, natural flavor, apocarotenal, and calcium disodium EDTA.

The House Italian Dressing contains soybean oil, corn cider vinegar, water, onion juice, salt, garlic juice, sugar, high fructose corn syrup, spices, and xanthan gum.

DUNKIN' DONUTS: Dunkin' Donuts said their ingredient listings are on their website. They indicate under Allergy Data if individual items contain eggs, fish, milk, or other ingredients.

A plain bagel contains enriched flour (flour, niacin, ferrous sulfate, thiamin mononitrate, riboflavin, folic acid), water, and high fructose corn syrup. It contains less than 2 percent of the following: degerminated yellow corn meal, salt, partially hydrogenated vegetable oil (soybean, cottonseed), rice flour, yeast, and dough conditioner (enzymes, datem, ascorbic acid, L-cysteine, and azodicarbonamide).

Under Allergy Data, neither eggs nor milk are indicated for Plain, Berry Berry, Blueberry, Cinnamon Raisin, Everything, Garlic, Onion, Poppyseed, Salsa, Salt, Sesame, or Wheat Bagels.

Honey is listed for Berry Berry, Blueberry, and Wheat Bagels. Their Biscuit contains milk.

Most baked goods appear to contain milk, eggs, or both. For example, the Sugar Raised Donut contains enriched flour (bleached wheat flour, malted barley flour, niacin, reduced iron, thiamin mononitrate, riboflavin, and folic acid), water, partially hydrogenated soybean oil, sugar, dextrose, yeast, and contains 2 percent or less of the following: salt, whey, soy flour, mono- and diglycerides, sodium acid pyrophosphate, baking soda, sodium stearoyl lactylate, soy lecithin, nonfat milk, cellulose gum, guar gum, annatto, turmeric, sodium caseinate, natural and artificial flavor, gum arabic, xanthan gum, and carrageenan.

EAT'N PARK: They indicated that their vegetarian foods include a Vegetable Stir-Fry, Gardenburger, Portobella Mushroom/Wild Rice Soup, and an extensive salad bar with lettuce, mixed greens, spring mix, tomatoes, olives, red peppers, green peppers, red onions, green onions, mushrooms, carrots, celery, radishes, broccoli, cauliflower, beets, olives, peas, and snow peas. They are able to prepare menu items differently upon request to accommodate special needs. Their "vegetarian" foods may be fried in oil that has been used to cook meat products and may be cooked on the same surface where meat is cooked. They do not know what type of enzyme is in their cheese.

FUDDRUCKERS: We did not receive a returned survey, but some of their locations carry a Garden Burger.

HOULIHAN'S: We did not receive a survey from this company, but they list vegetarian Asian Lettuce Wraps, Vegetarian Asian Chop Chop Salad, and Vegetarian Patty Melt on their website.

JACK IN THE BOX: When we contacted Jack in the Box, they said that the information on their website was the most current version of their ingredient statement at that time. Note that variations may occur from the use of regional suppliers, seasonal influences, manufacturing tolerances, minor differences in product assembly at the restaurant level, recipe revisions, and other factors.

The following information is taken from the Jack in the Box website: Their guacamole contains avocado, salt, sugar, onion, red bell pepper, sodium acid pyrophosphate, erythorbic acid (antioxidant), spices, xanthan gum, garlic, jalapeño peppers, dextrose, citric acid, corn syrup solids, partially hydrogenated soybean and/or cotton seed oil, and lime juice concentrate.

The pita bread contains enriched wheat flour, water, yeast, and salt. Their biscuits, onion rings, Country Ranch Sliced Almonds, croutons, and gourmet seasoned croutons contain dairy products. The Spicy Corn Sticks contain corn masa, soybean oil, spices, corn flour, salt, onion powder, potato flour, tomato powder, natural flavor (unspecified source), garlic powder, green bell pepper powder, extractives of paprika and other spices, and citric acid.

Their frying shortening has partially hydrogenated soybean oil and partially hydrogenated cottonseed oil with TBHQ and citric acid added to help protect flavor, and dimethylpolysiloxane, an antifoam agent added.

Depending on the use of regional suppliers, the French fried potatoes may contain potatoes, partially hydrogenated vegetable shortening (soybean oil and/or canola oil), modified food starch, rice flour, dextrin, wheat starch, corn starch, salt, leavening (sodium acid pyrophosphate, sodium bicarbonate), whey, xanthan gum, dextrose, and are cooked in their frying shortening. OR they may be made from potatoes, partially hydrogenated vegetable oil (soybean and/or canola oils), modified food starch, salt, corn dextrin, corn starch, tapioca dextrin, sugar, leavening (sodium acid pyrophosphate, sodium bicarbonate), guar gum, dextrose, sodium acid pyrophosphate (to maintain natural color), and are cooked in their frying shortening.

Their Potato Wedges contain potatoes, batter mix (wheat flour, corn starch, tapioca dextrin, modified food starch, salt, rice flour, sugar, sodium acid pyrophosphate, sodium bicarbonate, guar gum), partially hydrogenated soybean oil, and are cooked in their frying shortening.

We received an e-mail from a reader saying that several vegetarian friends eat Jack in the Box Tacos on a regular basis, and there is a rumor the tacos are vegetarian. According to the Jack in the Box website, their Taco/Monster Taco contains textured vegetable protein but also beef as the first ingredient.

KFC: KFC's website classifies their cole slaw (which contains egg yolk), biscuits (which contains milk products), and macaroni and cheese (which contains egg and dairy products) as ovo-lacto vegetarian. They told us that the enzyme in their cheese is vegetable/microbial derived.

The company reported that their mashed potatoes (contains dry milk solids) and corn are vegetarian. They also said their BBQ Baked Beans are now vegetarian. Note their website listed this item as non-vegetarian (contains pork flavors) in February 2004.

The gravy served with the mashed potatoes contains meat flavoring, but the gravy can be omitted from the order. The corn is served with butter. Some restaurants serve pasta or macaroni salad (which contains eggs), three bean salad, and potato salad.

KFC uses soybean oil containing up to 5 percent cottonseed oil for its frying. The potato wedges and French fries are cooked in oil used to prepare chicken.

The two breads served at KFC both contain dairy and egg products. These breads do not contain animal shortening.

The greens, red beans and rice, and green beans contain meat and/or meat flavorings. Side dishes vary from restaurant to restaurant, but those mentioned here are served in almost all KFC restaurants.

About 20 percent of all KFC restaurants have an all-you-can-eat buffet where hot vegetables are served. These vegetables may contain meat flavorings, but it varies from restaurant to restaurant. You will need to inquire about this at individual locations. The buffet also has a wide selection of salad fixings. Some stores may offer a garden salad.

KFC serves Little Bucket Parfaits for dessert. KFC states that the mono- and diglycerides in the Little Bucket Parfaits are derived from a vegetable source. The Cherry Cheesecake Parfait contains gelatin. All of the Little Bucket Parfaits contain eggs and dairy products.

Please note the disclaimer on the KFC website: "Please be aware, however, that some variations can be expected due to regional and seasonal differences in products, substitutions of ingredients, minor differences in product assembly on a restaurant-by-restaurant basis, and other factors."

KRISPY KREME DOUGHNUT: When asked about their vegetarian and vegan items, Krispy Kreme referred us to their website. Their website contains the following statement regarding animal products: "The only animal byproducts used in our doughnut are eggs (whites and yolks) and dairy products (including milk, butter, yogurt, whey, nonfat milk and nonfat whey). Our doughnuts are cooked in 100% vegetable oil shortening (partially hydrogenated soybean and/or cottonseed oil). All monoglycerides, diglycerides and enzymes are vegetable based. The lecithin we use is soy based. We also use wheat in our doughnuts, including bran, germ, gluten, starch and flour. Our products may contain allergens. To get further information about our products call us at (800) 4KRISPY."

LITTLE CAESARS: According to the company's website, "Little Caesars is proud to acknowledge that it offers many menu items that are suitable for vegetarians, even for those with the strictest standards.

"Little Caesars pizzas can be ordered with cheese-only or with any of our fresh vegetable toppings including onions, green peppers, and tomato slices. Mushrooms, ripe olives, and pineapples are also available toppings. And, banana pepper rings can be added to give some 'zip' to any vegetable-topped pizza."

According to their website, Little Caesars pizza crust is made with high-protein flour and contains no eggs or dairy-based conditioners. The sauce is made from crushed tomatoes and is made without animal broth or by-products.

Customers can order a vegetable pizza without cheese. Little Caesars recommends ordering your cheeseless pizza with a sesame-seed crust. At home, they suggest you serve your pizza with side dishes, such as seeds, nuts, or tofu. Also, their Crazy Bread can be ordered without Parmesan cheese along with an order of Crazy Sauce on the side.

Little Caesars menu products are subject to change, with or without notice.

MANHATTAN BAGEL CO: We weren't able to obtain a completed survey, but according to this company's website, their plain bagel contains high gluten flour, water, sugar, salt, yeast, and dough conditioners. Ingredients for other bagels are listed on their site.

McDonald's: In a May 2003 press release, Hain Celestial Group announced that it had partnered with McDonald's to create a soy-based patty for the McVeggie Burger®. Hain said the McVeggie Burger® is being manufactured exclusively for McDonald's by Yves Veggie Cuisine. Yves is a Hain brand which already produces many store products for vegetarians.

In September 2003, McDonald's informed us that the Mc-Veggie Burger® can be found on the chain's menu in Canada and that they were testing it in southern California, New York, and Houston. Yves makes the McVeggie Burger® for southern California restaurants and will also produce this item for Houston and Oregon. The patty's ingredients are: water, soy protein product, partially hydrogenated soybean oil, vital wheat gluten, modified cellulose, spices, salt, evaporated cane juice powder, hydrolyzed corn and soy protein, natural flavor (vegetable source), yeast extract, caramel color, vitamin B1 (thiamine hydrochloride), vitamin B2 (riboflavin), vitamin B3 (niacinamide), vitamin B6 (pyridoxine hydrochloride), vitamin B12 (cyano-cobalamin), pantothenic acid (calcium pantothenate), reduced iron, and zinc (zinc oxide).

This burger comes on a whole wheat bun made from the following ingredients: whole wheat flour, water, cracked wheat, high fructose corn syrup, vegetable oil (partially hydrogenated soybean oil), gluten, yeast, salt, calcium sulfate, DATEM (diacetyl tartaric acid ester of mono-diglycerides), distilled monoglycerides, calcium propionate (preservative), azodicarbonamide, and fungal enzymes. It is served with a tomato slice, lettuce, chopped onions, barbeque sauce, and pickles.

The McVeggie Burgers® are cooked on the same surfaces as the meat products and cannot be microwaved. The following disclaimers are found on the McDonald's website: "While the ingredient information is based on standard product formulations, variations may occur depending on the local supplier, the region of the country and the season of the year. Further, product formulations change periodically. No products are certified as vegetarian; all products may contain trace amounts of ingredients derived from animals."

Customer service wrote that these disclaimers applied to all their menu items, including the McVeggie Burger® and the whole wheat bun. In December, 2003, McDonald's stated on their website that "McDonald's does not represent any of their foods as being vegetarian."

Note that the McVeggie Burger® in Canada is assembled differently than in the United States The McVeggie Burger® in New York was developed by an owner/operator and is produced by a different company (which produces other vegetarian and non-vegetarian items). Ingredient information was not available at the time of publication.

Although none of their products are certified as vegetarian, the McDonald's representative suggested several meatless choices, such as the side salad, some premium salads without chicken, and the fruit and yogurt parfait.

We asked if the English muffins, scrambled eggs, hotcakes, cinnamon rolls, bagels, biscuits, McGriddle cakes, or apple pies are cooked/fried in oil that has been used to cook meat/chicken/seafood products. McDonald's responded that, "While cross-contamination of products is avoided, all products may contain trace amounts of ingredients derived from animals."

In addition, we asked if McDonald's yogurt parfaits, ice creams, sundaes, McFlurries, or shakes contain gelatin (animal-derived protein). McDonald's responded, "While gelatin, per se, is not listed as an ingredient, ingredient information is based on standard product formulations, and variations may occur depending on the local supplier, the region of the country and the season of the year. Product formulations may change periodically."

When asked about the enzymes in their cheese, they responded, "Cheese is purchased from suppliers who also provide cheese available in supermarkets. The enzyme used in cheese-making is determined by the cheese manufacturer."

Customers can visit the website <www.mcdonalds.com> to learn specific nutritional values and ingredients used in their menu. For example, the website states McDonald's French fries contain: potatoes, partially hydrogenated soybean oil, natural flavor (beef source), dextrose, sodium acid pyrophosphate (to preserve natural color). They are cooked in partially hydro-genated vegetable oils (may contain partially hydrogenated soybean oil and/or partially hydrogenated corn oil and/or partially hydrogenated canola oil and/or cottonseed oil and/or sunflower oil and/or corn oil). TBHQ and citric acid are added to help preserve freshness. Dimethylpolysiloxane is added as an anti-foaming agent. Their Hash Browns also contain a beef source natural flavor.

Their bagel contains enriched bleached wheat flour (malted barley flour, niacin, iron, thiamine mononitrate, riboflavin, folic acid), water, propylene glycol, brown sugar, salt, yeast, dough conditioner (flour, monocalcium phosphate, corn starch, salt, mono- and diglycerides [from vegetable sources], ascorbic acid, potassium & calcium iodate, enzyme, azodicarbonamide).

Their Baked Apple Pie contains apples, corn syrup, sugar, water, modified corn starch, sorbitol, dextrose, brown sugar, sodium alginate, spices, citric acid, salt, dicalcium phosphate. The pastry consists of enriched bleached wheat flour, vegetable shortening (partially hydrogenated soybean and/or cottonseed oil), water, sugar, salt, yeast, l-cysteine (dough conditioner), and lecithin. The topping contains sugar, spice, and partially hydrogenated soybean oil.

NATHAN'S: Their website says that they cook their potatoes in 100 percent cholesterol-free corn oil.

OLIVE GARDEN: We did not receive a survey back from Olive Garden. On their website, they call their Minestrone "a vegetarian classic."

OUTBACK STEAK HOUSE: According to Outback, vegan alternatives would include house salad (without cheese or croutons), baked potatoes, sweet potatoes, veggie griller (substitute a potato for the rice), steamed veggies (without seasoned butter), and dry pasta with steamed veggies (without butter). The fries are cooked in tallow, and the soups are made with a chicken stock. Outback said they cook their meals from scratch, so it is no problem to meet most special requests with regard to preparation.

PAPA JOHN'S: Papa John's states that neither their pizza dough nor sauce contains animal products, and according to their website, there are no eggs in their pizza ingredients.

The ingredients listed for the pizza dough include: unbleached enriched wheat flour (niacin, iron [reduced], thiamine mononitrate, riboflavin, folic acid), malted barley flour, clear filtered water, sugar, soybean oil, salt, yeast, ascorbic acid (added as dough conditioner), enzymes. The Thin Crust contains flour (wheat flour, malted barley flour), water, partially hydrogenated soybean oil, yeast, salt, and calcium propionate (preservative). Neither their original dough nor Thin Crust contains animal shortening or lard.

The 6" Pan Pizza Shells contain enriched flour (bleached wheat flour, malted barley flour, niacin, ferrous sulfate, thiamin mononitrate, riboflavin, folic acid), water, soybean oil, shortening (partially hydrogenated vegetable oil, soybean and/or cottonseed oils), olive oil, yeast, salt, sugar, glycerin, wheat starch, and L-cysteine.

Papa John's Pizza Sauce contains tomatoes, blend of vegetable oils (sunflower and olive), sugar, salt, garlic, spices, citric acid, and soybean oil. Their banana peppers contain polysorbate 80.

Their cheese is made with a biosynthesized enzyme called Chymax®. Their Parmesan cheese shaker and cheese dipping sauce contain animal derived enzymes. They are able to prepare meatless pizzas. Their pizza items are not fried. Their meatless pizzas are cooked in the same ovens as other non-vegetarian pizzas.

The Special Garlic Sauce contains liquid margarine (partially hydrogenated soybean oil, water, salt, mono- and diglycerides, lecithin, sodium benzoate [a preservative], calcium disodium EDTA and citric acid [to protect flavor], colored with beta carotene, vitamin A palmitate added), water, garlic powder, salt, lactic acid (manufactured from a microbiological fermentation of *lactobacillus* sp. Bacteria), natural garlic flavor. However, the Special Garlic Sauce can be made from liquid and partially hydrogenated soybean oil, water, salt, dehydrated garlic, vegetable mono- and diglycerides, soy lecithin, natural garlic flavor, artificial flavor, sodium benzoate (a preservative), lactic acid, calcium disodium EDTA (added to protect flavor), beta carotene (color), vitamin A palmitate added, and citric acid.

The Buffalo Dipping Sauce contains hot sauce (cayenne pepper, distilled vinegar, salt, garlic), soybean oil, xanthan gum, and spices.

PIZZA HUT: At this time, the company has decided not to participate in our survey. Although there may be a few items on their menu that are incidentally vegetarian or vegan, they do not want to state that any of their items are vegetarian or vegan. They do not want to mislead customers in any way. Interested customers may write to customer service about specific ingredients. (Please contact The VRG if you receive additional information or updates.)

According to the Pizza Hut website in June 2003, some products may contain ingredients which some consumers choose to avoid, such as enzymes, sugar, or salt. Previously, Pizza Hut has indicated to us that they use microbial rennet in their cheese. However, they have not sent us a current written statement either way.

Pizza Hut restaurants in Ft. Wayne, Indiana, were testing soy cheese at more than 40 locations. This is not a vegan item.

PIZZA PRO: Pizza Pro offers a vegetable or cheese pizza, and they said they are able to meet special requests.

Their pizza crust is free of milk, eggs, and honey. When asked about rennin, they said no animal derivatives are used in the making of their cheese. (If you are concerned about this, you should consult with the company.) Cinnamon sticks are also on the menu. They are made from pizza dough and sprinkled with cinnamon and sugar. They are basted with liquid margarine.

Their foods may contain natural flavors which are animal-derived. They said their vegetarian foods are cooked on the same surfaces as non-vegetarian foods. All products are baked, and they do not fry foods.

RED LOBSTER: Red Lobster did not return a survey to us. However, their website says that, while they do not have vegetarian items on their menu, some items can be prepared without meat or seafood. Speak with the manager about how your needs can be met.

RUBY TUESDAY'S: They've tested a vegan burger from Veggie-Land™ and a vegetarian Garden Burger.

SBARRO: Sbarro reports that there are no animal products in its dough or pizza sauce and that vegetarian rennet is used in the cheeses. They stated other vegetarian menu items include garden salad, fruit salad, rice, and vegetables.

SUBWAY: According to the Subway website, in the United States, the Subway Italian bread contains no animal-derived ingredients. The wheat bread and deli roll contain honey, but no other animal-derived ingredients. The sodium stearoyl-2-lactylate and the mono- and diglycerides in the bread are plant-derived.

Subway's website also reports that the bulk of rennet used in processing their cheese is microbial; however, there could be a chance of calf rennin in the cheese due to production variables.

The company said the menu items that do not contain any animal-derived ingredients include the Veggie Delite® on Italian bread and the Veggie Delite® salad. Also, these individual items do not contain animal-derived ingredients: all vegetables, oil, vinegar, mustard, sweet onion sauce, and Fruizle.

Considering Subway's apparent openess in providing vegan information, it is interesting that the company is the fifth largest chain ranked by food service sales, according to the National Restaurant Association. Subway states that they have more locations than McDonald's.

TACO BELL: If requested, Taco Bell will send a list of their menu items that are suitable for vegetarians.

Under their lacto-ovo heading, they list the following: Pintos & Cheese, Bean Burrito, Bean Tostada, Mexican Rice, Seven Layer Burrito (without sour cream), Cheese, Gordita Shells, Creamy Jalapeño Sauce, Creamy Lime Sauce, Pepper Jack Sauce, Baja Sauce, Fiesta Salsa, Red Sauce, Hot/Mild/Fire Sauce, Green Sauce, Pizza Sauce, Guacamole, and Taco Shell.

Under their vegan heading, they list Bean Burrito (without cheese), Bean Tostada (without cheese), Mexican Rice (without cheese), Seven Layer Burrito (without sour cream or cheese), Hot/Mild/Fire Sauce, Fiesta Salsa, Red Sauce, Soft Tortillas, Pizza Sauce, Green Sauce, Guacamole, and Taco Shell.

Taco Bell used to have two different distributors for the Mexican Rice. They are no longer using the distributor which had milk derivatives in the rice.

Taco Bell indicates that their cheese is vegetarian. The company writes, "Historically, enzymes used in the production of cheese were of an animal source. The enzyme, rennet, contains a micro-organism called chymosin. Chymosin is the actual agent that causes the state change from liquid to semi-solid (coagulation). Today, due to the need for Kosher cheese and the cost of using animal sources, genetically engineered coagulants are used. The genetically engineered chymosin is derived from a modified strain of the dairy yeast *Kluyveromyces lactis*. It is formulated to coagulate the milk so we can make our cheese without the use of animal coagulants."

NOTE that the sour cream does contain gelatin, which is animal based.

The Chalupa Shells, Nacho Chips, Cinnamon Twists, and Potato Nuggets are fried at individual restaurants, and the same oil is used for the Crispy Red Strips. The Crispy Red Strips contain carmine. Carmine is derived commercially from insects. The Chalupa Shells contain nonfat dry milk powder.

The Nacho Chips are made of white corn flour, water, fumaric acid, cellulose gum, preservatives (sodium propionate, sorbic acid), and a trace of lime. The oil is partially hydrogenated soybean oil with dimethylpolysiloxane, an antifoaming agent added.

The Cinnamon Twists consist of wheat flour, yellow corn flour, rice flour, and salt. The Cinnamon Sugar consists of sugar, cinnamon, dextrin, and extractives of cinnamon. The oil is partially hydrogenated soybean oil with dimethylpolysiloxane, an antifoaming agent added.

The Potato Nuggets (not available at all locations) are made of potatoes, vegetable shortening (contains one or more of the following: partially hydrogenated soybean and/or canola oils), salt, dextrose, and disodium dihydrogen pyrophosphate (to maintain natural color).

According to a telephone statement from Taco Bell, the Taco and Tostada Shells are vegan and are fried by the distributors, not at the store level. The Tostada Shell contains corn, vegetable oil (may contain one or all of the following: soybean, corn or cottonseed oil), and TBHQ (used as a preservative).

Over the telephone, they also said that the new menu item "Cheesy Bean & Rice Burrito" can be made vegan if ordered without cheese, nacho sauce, and jalapeño sauce (Zesty Sauce). This burrito does not come with sour cream. Taco Bell said the nacho sauce has some colorings that may not be acceptable to some vegetarians.

There are three different versions of the Flour Tortilla. One version included enriched bleached wheat flour (flour, malted barley, niacin, reduced iron, thiamin mononitrate, riboflavin, and folic acid), water, partially hydrogenated shortening (soybean and/or cottonseed oil, which may contain mono- and diglycerides). This flour contains 2 percent or less of the following: salt, baking powder (sodium acid pyrophosphate and/or sodium aluminum sulfate), sodium bicarbonate, starch, monocalcium phosphate), sugar, sodium bicarbonate, DATEM, fumaric acid, potassium sorbate, calcium propionate (used as preservatives), and enzymes.

Their beans contain pinto beans, partially hydrogenated corn oil (freshness preserved with TBHQ), salt, calcium chloride, artificial color, and red no. 40; or, from a different supplier, pinto beans, partially hydrogenated corn oil (with TBHQ to preserve freshness), and salt.

The Creamy Guacamole contains Hass avocado, water, sugar, lemon juice concentrate, salt, jalapeño pepper purée (jalapeño peppers, salt, acetic acid, and a trace of calcium chloride), dehydrated onion, sodium alginate, dehydrated garlic, white pepper, erythorbic acid (to maintain natural color), xanthan gum, and citric acid.

Taco Bell stressed that while the ingredients listed above may be categorized as acceptable for certain types of vegetarian diets, all ingredients are handled by employees in common with other ingredients which may not be acceptable to certain types of vegetarian diets.

Menu offerings may vary regionally.

TACO DEL MAR: Taco Del Mar states that these menu items are vegetarian: veggie tacos, veggie burritos, veggie taco salads, cheese quesadilla, and rice and beans. However, they said that the enzyme used in the cheese is unknown. All their beans are vegetarian.

The company indicates that the vegan burrito, salsa, and guacamole are vegan. The tortilla chips are made with one or more of the following oils: corn oil, cottonseed oil, canola oil, or sunflower oil.

At Taco Del Mar, the vegetarian and vegan menu items are cooked in soybean oil, and this oil is not shared with meat/chicken/seafood products. Vegetarian and vegan menu items are not cooked on the same surfaces that are used to cook meat/chicken/seafood products. The beans are kept separate from meat protein.

Taco Del Mar is happy to prepare menu items differently upon request. For example, they can omit meat, cheese, and sour cream from any menu item.

T.G.I. Friday's: T.G.I. Friday's says the following menu items are vegetarian: spinach dip, fried mozzarella, vegetable grill, garden burger, roasted vegetable sandwich, and strawberry fields salad. They state that the enzyme used in their cheeses is microbial. Also, they say that the vegetable grill is vegan and that the roasted vegetable sandwich and strawberry fields salad are vegan if ordered without the cheese.

T.G.I. Friday's reports that, if vegetarian or vegan foods are fried, they use soybean oil. If the foods are deep-fried, the oil may have been used to cook meat items. However, if the vegetarian/vegan foods are sautéed, they are not cooked in the same oil as meat items.

The natural flavoring for the French fries does not come from an animal source. However, some of their sauces may contain animal-derived ingredients.

Their baked goods do not contain animal shortening or lard. None are free of milk, eggs, and/or their derivatives. T.G.I. Friday's was not sure if any of their products contained gelatin.

T.G.I Friday's is able to prepare menu items differently upon request to accommodate a vegetarian diet or other special dietary needs.

WENDY'S: Wendy's reports that the following menu items are vegetarian: broccoli and cheese baked potato, spring mix salad, side salad, Frosties, soft drinks, and all the salad dressings except the Caesar's and Reduced Fat Creamy Ranch Dressing.

They said that their plain baked potato is vegan, although margarine and sour cream packets are provided as condiments. The margarine contains whey, and the mono- and diglycerides that are used in their foods may not be suitable for vegetarians or vegans. Their sour cream and reduced fat creamy ranch dressing contain animal-derived gelatin.

Their honey roasted pecans contain pecans, sucrose, soybean oil, wheat starch, maltodextrin, honey, lactose, salt, and xanthan gum. They may contain trace amounts of peanuts and other nuts.

The American cheese slices and cheese sauce contain bacterial and natural animal-derived enzymes. The shredded cheddar cheese contains bacterial enzymes; however, the supplier could not give a 100 percent guarantee that there were no animal-derived enzymes in the cheese. The Parmesan cheese contains rennet. The Ranch Dipping Sauce contains natural flavors that are animal-derived.

Partially hydrogenated corn and soybean oils are used for frying, not animal-derived oils or fat.

The French fries consist of potatoes, partially hydrogenated soybean oil, dextrose, and disodium dihydrogen pyrophosphate (retains color). They contain no natural flavors that are animal-derived and are cooked in partially hydrogenated corn and soybean oil. However, they may be cooked in the same oil as chicken nuggets and chicken strips.

Wendy's will prepare their sandwiches without the meat. The Kaiser and sandwich buns contain: enriched and bleached flour (wheat flour, thiamin mononitrate, riboflavin, niacin, iron, folic acid), water, high fructose corn syrup, partially hydrogenated soybean oil, yeast, salt, and vital wheat gluten. It contains less than 2 percent of each of the following: sodium stearoyl lactylate and calcium stearoyl-2-lactylate (dough conditioners), colored with turmeric and paprika, calcium sulfate, yellow corn meal (Kaiser bun only), calcium propionate (preservative), distilled monoglycerides, soy flour, ascorbic acid, azodicarbonamide, and DATEM (dough conditioners).

There is no monosodium glutamate (MSG) in any of the foods served at Wendy's, nor is there hydrolyzed vegetable protein, a vegan ingredient which contains salt and monosodium glutamate.

Variations in foods may occur due to differences in suppliers, ingredient substitutions, recipe revisions, product assembly at the restaurant level, and/or season of the year. Wendy's does not assume responsibility for a particular sensitivity or allergy to any food provided in their restaurants. They encourage anyone with food sensitivities, allergies, or special dietary needs to call or write their Consumer Relations Department to obtain the most up-to-date information.

WHATABURGER: In June 2003, a reader told us that a Boca Burger was being offered in the Austin market.

According to the Whataburger website, their wheat buns contain: unbleached enriched wheat flour, water, high fructose corn syrup, whole wheat flour, yeast, partially hydrogenated soybean oil or soybean oil or canola oil, wheat gluten, salt, wheat bran, nonfat milk, molasses, dough conditioners, soy flour, calcium sulfate, calcium propionate, caramel color, monocalcium phosphate, and ammonium sulfate. The dough conditioners contain sodium stearoyl lactylate, calcium stearol-2-lactylate, and monoglycerides, which are made from vegetable sources. The conditioners also contain calcium iodate and calcium peroxide.

The flour tortillas contain enriched bleached wheat flour, water, vegetable shortening, salt, leavening (baking soda, sodium acid pyrophosphate), calcium propionate and sorbic acid (to preserve freshness), and dough conditioners (fumaric acid and L-cysteine).

Their French Fries contain: potatoes, partially hydrogenated vegetable oil (canola oil and/or soybean oil), dextrose, and sodium acid pyrophosphate added to preserve natural color. The French fries are deep fried in Whataburger Liquid Shortening. Their liquid frying shortening contains partially hydrogenated soybean oil, TBHQ and citric acid, and dimethylpolysiloxane. The Hashbrown Sticks contain natural flavoring. The origin isn't indicated. Onion rings contain nonfat milk, egg white, and natural flavor.

Their Fried Apple Turnover contains water, enriched flour, apples, sugar, partially hydrogenated vegetable shortening, modified food starch, corn syrup, high fructose corn syrup, salt, soy flour, leavening (disodium dihydrogen pyrophosphate, sodium bicarbonate), spices, dextrose, natural and artificial flavoring, erythorbic acid and/or citric acid and/or ascorbic acid, and caramel color. The Turnover is deep-fried in Whataburger Liquid Shortening.

Their buttermilk biscuits, croutons, pancakes, and cinnamon rolls contain dairy ingredients.

The Vegetarian Resource Group has been providing information on restaurant chains for more than 18 years. Special thanks to Heather Gorn, John Cunningham, Keryl Cryer, and Jeannie McStay for their help with this edition.

Readers should let us know if they hear of any new vegetarian items being offered at restaurant chains. Write to VRG, P.O. Box 1463, Baltimore, MD 21203. Our e-mail address is vrg@vrg.org, and our website is <www.vrg.org>.

ONCE AGAIN, PLEASE NOTE: We depend on company statements for product and ingredient information. It is impossible to be 100 percent sure about a statement, information can change, people have different views, and mistakes can be made. Please use your own best judgement about whether a product is suitable for you. To be certain, do further research or confirmation on your own. If you want to be 100 percent sure, we suggest you do not eat items from these establishments. If you are like the majority of Americans, please do the best you can.

The contents of this handout and our other publications, including web information, are not intended to provide personal medical advice. Medical advice should be obtained from a qualified health professional.

Low-Cost Quick and Easy Vegan Menus Using Convenience Foods

By Reed Mangels, PhD, RD

Many of us would like to spend less time cooking. If you know what to buy and have some quick-to-prepare ideas, you can have "convenience food" on a budget. We've developed menus using a combination of easy-to-fix meals that are quick, inexpensive, and healthful.

The first set of menus was devised to meet the needs of those aged 19-50 years. The menus for women have around 2,200 calories per day, while the men's menus are around 2,500 calories. If you are very active, you will need more calories. You have several choices; you can eat more of the foods already on the menus, or you can add favorite foods to the menus. Conversely, if you are not very active or wish to lose excess weight, you will need fewer calories. In that case, we recommend cutting out some of the "extras" like margarine, chips, desserts, and vegan mayonnaise.

The menus were planned to meet the average person's needs for most nutrients over a week-long period. Although these menus provide generous amounts of iron, women may require additional iron in the form of an iron supplement.

We used specific brand names of foods but have included information on other foods that can be substituted if you don't care for a particular food.

We were curious about how costly these menus would be. The average cost for 1 day's food for a man was a bit over $6 using conventional fruits and vegetables and around $8 using all organic products. The average cost for one day's food for a woman was around $5.50 using conventional fruits and vege-tables and almost $7.50 using all organic products. Pricing was done in the winter in New England, so costs may vary depending on the season, your location, and inflation. If you want to reduce food costs even more, you can buy products when they are on sale; see if your supermarket will offer case discounts for items you use often like soymilk. Also, consider buying store brands instead of name brands, use coupons, and choose fruits and vegetables that are in season.

Day 1 for Female, 19-50 years old

Breakfast:
- 1/2 cup calcium-fortified orange juice
- 1 medium banana
- 2 slices whole-wheat toast with 1 Tablespoon nut butter (peanut, almond, cashew, etc.)
- 1 cup Wheat Chex cereal or any vegan fortified cereal providing 20% of the DV for iron or more per cup
- 1 cup Soy Dream Enriched soymilk

Lunch:
- 1 bowl of Fantastic Foods Big Bowl of Noodles and Hot and Sour Soup or any soup/entrée cup providing 250-300 calories/cup and at least 8% of the DV for iron per serving such as Health Valley Pasta Italiano Soup or Health Valley Lentil with Couscous Soup
- 10 saltines with 1 Tablespoon nut butter (peanut, almond, cashew, etc.)
- 1 medium orange
- 1/2 cup carrot sticks

Dinner:
- 1 Morningstar Farms Harvest Burger on a bun or any burger providing at least 15% of the DV for iron such as 2 Whole Foods Vegan Burgers with a large slice of tomato
- 1 medium baked potato

Snack:
- 1 cup Soy Dream Enriched soymilk
- 1 cup kidney beans mixed with 1 Tablespoon salsa served with 1 ounce lowfat tortilla chips

Day 2 for Female, 19-50 years old

Breakfast:
- 1 bagel with 2 teaspoons vegan margarine
- 1 medium orange
- 1 cup Cheerios cereal or any vegan fortified cereal providing 20% of the DV for iron or more per cup
- 1 cup Soy Dream Enriched soymilk

Lunch:
- Sandwich of hummus made with 3/4 cup chickpeas and 2 teaspoons tahini on 2 slices of whole-wheat bread with 3 slices of tomato
- 1 medium apple

Dinner:
- 1 cup of cooked pasta with 1/4 cup marinara sauce
- 1/3 cup carrot sticks
- 1 cup cooked broccoli (frozen or fresh)
- 1 whole-wheat roll
- Juice pop made with 1 cup frozen grape juice

Snack:
- 1/2 cup trail mix (mix of nuts, raisins, and sunflower seeds)
- 1 cup Soy Dream Enriched soymilk

Note: In all the menus, Soy Dream Enriched soymilk can be replaced with Silk soymilk or any other calcium-fortified soymilk that provides at least 25% of the Daily Value (DV) for vitamin D and 20% of the DV for vitamin B12 in an 8-ounce serving.

Day 3 for Female, 19-50 years old

Breakfast:

Scrambled tofu made with 1/2 cup tofu, 1/4 cup onions, and 1 teaspoon oil

1 cup calcium-fortified orange juice

2 slices whole-wheat toast with 2 teaspoons vegan margarine

Lunch:

Sandwich made with 1 large pita bread, 1/2 cup shredded lettuce, 1/4 cup chopped tomato, 1/4 cup grated carrot, and 1 Tablespoon Nayonnaise or any spread providing 25-50 calories or can be omitted

Fantastic Foods Country Lentil soup cup or any soup cup providing 200-300 calories and at least 30% of the DV for iron

1 medium banana

1 cup Soy Dream Enriched soymilk

Dinner:

1/2 cup kidney beans with 1 cup cooked quick brown rice and 2 Tablespoons salsa

1 cup frozen mashed squash

1 cup unsweetened applesauce

Snack:

1/2 cup trail mix (mix of nuts, raisins, and sunflower seeds)

1 cup Soy Dream Enriched soymilk

Day 4 for Female, 19-50 years old

<u>Breakfast</u>:
>   1-1/2 cups cooked quick oats with 3 Tablespoons wheat
>   germ, 1/4 cup raisins, and 1 ounce chopped walnuts
>   1 cup diced cantaloupe
>   1 cup Soy Dream Enriched soymilk

<u>Lunch</u>:
>   Burrito made with 1 Garden of Eatin' whole-wheat tortilla
>   or any tortilla providing 125-150 calories and 6% of the
>   DV for iron, 1/2 cup black beans, and 1 Tablespoon
>   salsa
>   1 ounce lowfat tortilla chips served with 1/4 cup salsa

<u>Dinner</u>:
>   6 ounces calcium-fortified V-8 juice
>   Stir-fry made with 1/2 cup diced tofu, 1 cup frozen stir-fry
>   vegetables, 2 Tablespoons soy sauce, 1-1/2 cups
>   cooked quick brown rice, and 1 teaspoon oil
>   3 graham crackers

<u>Snack</u>:
>   1 cup Soy Dream Enriched soymilk
>   3 cups popped popcorn sprinkled with 1 Tablespoon
>   Vegetarian Support Formula nutritional yeast

Day 5 for Female, 19-50 years old

Breakfast:
    1 English muffin with 1 Tablespoon jelly
    1 cup calcium-fortified orange juice

Lunch:
    Baked tofu made with 4 ounces tofu and 1 Tablespoon
        soy sauce
    1 large sweet potato
    1 Imagine Foods Chocolate Pudding Cup or any product
        providing 120-200 calories such as other flavors of
        Imagine pudding cups, ZenDon soy pudding cup, 2
        Sweet Nothings Bars, 2 Soy Dream Lil' Dreams, 2 Whole
        Foods Frozen Fruit Bars, or 1/2 cup frozen dessert

Dinner:
    1 Yves the Good Dog or any vegan hot dogs providing
        75-90 calories, at least 20% of the DV for iron, and at least
        3% of the DV for zinc such as 2 Yves Tofu Dogs
    1 cup vegetarian baked beans
    1-1/2 cups cooked kale (frozen or fresh)
    2 tomato slices
    1 bagel
    1 baked apple made with 1 medium apple, 1/4 cup
        chopped dates, and 1 Tablespoon granulated sweetener
    1 cup Soy Dream Enriched soymilk

Snack:
    1 ounce walnuts
    1/4 cup raisins
    1 cup Soy Dream Enriched soymilk

Day 6 for Female, 19-50 years old

Breakfast:
- 1 cup Wheat Chex cereal or any vegan fortified cereal providing 20% of the DV for iron or more per cup with 1 medium peach, sliced, and 1 cup Soy Dream Enriched soymilk
- 2 slices whole-wheat toast

Lunch:
- 1 sandwich made with 2 slices whole-wheat bread, 2 Tablespoons nut butter (peanut, almond, cashew, etc.), and 1 Tablespoon jelly
- 1/3 cup carrot sticks
- 1 cup grapes
- 1 cup Soy Dream Enriched soymilk

Dinner:
- 1/2 cup kidney beans with 1 cup cooked pasta and 1/2 cup marinara sauce
- 1 Garden of Eatin' whole-wheat tortilla or any tortilla providing 125-150 calories and 6% of the DV for iron
- 1 medium orange
- 1 cup cooked collard greens (frozen or fresh)

Snack:
- 1 kiwi fruit
- 1/4 cup soynuts
- 10 whole-wheat crackers

Don't forget, although these menus provide generous amounts of iron, women may require additional iron in the form of an iron supplement.

Day 7 for Female, 19-50 years old

Breakfast:
>1-1/2 cups cooked quick oats with 2 Tablespoons wheat
>germ
>1 English muffin with 2 teaspoons vegan margarine
>1 cup calcium-fortified apple juice

Lunch:
>Sandwich made with 2 slices whole-wheat bread,
>2 ounces Yves Veggie Bologna Slices or any deli slice
>providing 50-100 calories and 20% of the DV for iron in a
>serving such as Lightlife's Smart Deli Bologna Style (3
>slices) or Yves Veggie Salami Slices (4 slices), 1 Table-
>spoon Nayonnaise or any spread providing 25-50
>calories or omitted, 1/3 cup shredded lettuce, and 2
>slices tomato
>1 wedge watermelon
>1 cup Soy Dream Enriched soymilk

Dinner:
>1/2 cup chickpeas and 3/4 cup peas with 1 Tablespoon
>tahini on 1-1/2 cups cooked couscous
>Smoothie made with 1 cup Soy Dream Enriched soymilk,
>3 ounces soft tofu, 1 medium frozen banana, 1/2 cup
>strawberries, and 1 Tablespoon maple syrup

Snack:
>Hummus made with 1/3 cup chickpeas and 1 teaspoon
>tahini
>1/3 cup carrot sticks
>1/2 cup celery

Day 1 for Male, 19-50 years old

Breakfast:
- 1 cup calcium-fortified orange juice
- 1 medium banana
- 2 slices whole-wheat toast with 1 Tablespoon nut butter (peanut, almond, cashew, etc.)
- 1 cup Wheat Chex cereal or any vegan ready-to-eat cereal
- 1 cup Soy Dream Enriched soymilk

Lunch:
- 1 bowl of Fantastic Foods Big Bowl of Noodles and Hot and Sour Soup or any soup/entrée cup providing 250-300 calories/cup such as Fantastic Foods Big Bowl of Italian Tomato Noodle, Health Valley Pasta Italiano Soup, or Health Valley Lentil with Couscous Soup
- 10 saltines with 2 Tablespoons nut butter (peanut, almond, cashew, etc.)
- 1 medium orange
- 1/2 cup carrot sticks

Dinner:
- 1 Morningstar Farms Harvest Burger or any vegan burger such as Whole Foods 365 Vegan Burger, Lightlife Meatless Lightburgers, Boca Vegan Burger, Gardenburger Garden Vegan, or Amy's California Burger on a bun with a large slice of tomato
- 1 large baked potato

Snack:
- 1 cup Soy Dream Enriched soymilk
- 1 cup of kidney beans mashed with 1 Tablespoon salsa
- 1 ounce lowfat tortilla chips

Day 2 for Male, 19-50 years old

Breakfast:
  1 bagel with 2 teaspoons vegan margarine
  1 medium orange
  1 cup Wheat Chex cereal or any vegan ready-to-eat cereal
  1 cup Soy Dream Enriched soymilk
Lunch:
  2 hummus sandwiches made with 3/4 cup chickpeas and
    2 teaspoons tahini on 4 slices of whole-wheat bread with
    3 slices of tomato
  1 medium apple
Dinner:
  1 cup cooked pasta with 1/4 cup marinara sauce
  1/3 cup carrot sticks
  1 cup cooked broccoli (frozen or fresh)
  2 whole-wheat rolls
  2 teaspoons vegan margarine
  Juice pop made with 1 cup frozen grape juice
Snack:
  1/2 cup trail mix (mix of nuts, raisins, sunflower seeds)
  1 cup Soy Dream Enriched soymilk

Note: In all the menus, Soy Dream Enriched soymilk can be re-placed with Silk soymilk or any other calcium-fortified soymilk that provides at least 25% of the Daily Value (DV) for vitamin D and 20% of the DV for vitamin B12 in an 8-ounce serving.

Day 3 for Male, 19-50 years old

Breakfast:
  1 cup calcium-fortified orange juice
  Scrambled tofu made with 1/2 cup tofu, 1/4 cup onions, and 2 teaspoons oil
  2 slices whole-wheat toast with 2 teaspoons vegan margarine

Lunch:
  Sandwich made with 1-1/2 large whole-wheat pitas filled with 1/2 cup shredded lettuce, 1/4 cup chopped tomato, 1/4 cup grated carrots, and 1 Tablespoon Nayonnaise or any vegan spread providing 25-50 calories or can be omitted
  Fantastic Foods Country Lentil soup cup or any soup cup providing 200-300 calories such as Fantastic Foods Cha-Cha Chili, Black Bean Soup, Split Pea Soup, Couscous with Lentils Soup, Five Bean Soup; or Health Valley Black Bean Soup or Chili
  1 medium banana
  1 cup Soy Dream Enriched soymilk

Dinner:
  3/4 cup kidney beans with 1 cup quick brown rice and 2 Tablespoons salsa
  1 Garden of Eatin' whole-wheat tortilla or any tortilla providing 125-150 calories per tortilla
  1 cup frozen mashed squash
  1 cup unsweetened applesauce

Snack:
  1/2 cup trail mix (mix of nuts, raisins, sunflower seeds)
  1 cup Soy Dream Enriched soymilk

Day 4 for Male, 19-50 years old

Breakfast:
- 1-1/2 cups quick rolled oats with 2 Tablespoons wheat germ, 1/4 cup chopped dates, and 1 ounce chopped walnuts
- 1 cup diced cantaloupe
- 2 slices whole-wheat toast with 1 Tablespoon nut butter (peanut, almond, cashew, etc.)
- 1 cup Soy Dream Enriched soymilk

Lunch:
- Burrito made with 1 Garden of Eatin' whole-wheat tortilla or any tortilla providing 125-150 calories per tortilla, 1/2 cup black beans, and 1 Tablespoon salsa
- 1 ounce lowfat tortilla chips
- 1/4 cup salsa
- 1 medium apple

Dinner:
- 6 ounces calcium-fortified V-8 juice
- Stir-fry made with 1/2 cup tofu cubes, 1 cup frozen stir-fry vegetable mix, 2 Tablespoons soy sauce, 1 teaspoon oil, and 1-1/2 cups cooked quick brown rice
- 3 graham crackers

Snack:
- 1 cup Soy Dream Enriched soymilk
- 3 cups popped popcorn with 1 Tablespoon Vegetarian Support Formula nutritional yeast

Day 5 for Male, 19-50 years old

Breakfast:
    1 vegan English muffin with 1 Tablespoon jelly
    1 cup grape juice
Lunch:
    Baked tofu made with 4 ounces sliced tofu and 1
        Tablespoon soy sauce
    1 large sweet potato
    1 Imagine Foods Chocolate Pudding Cup or any product
        providing 120-200 calories such as other flavors of
        Imagine pudding cups, ZenDon soy pudding cup, 2
        Sweet Nothings Bars, 2 Soy Dream Lil' Dreams, 2 Whole
        Foods Frozen Fruit Bars, or 1/2 cup frozen dessert
Dinner:
    2 Yves the Good Dogs or any vegan dogs providing 150-
        180 calories and at least 3% of the DV for zinc such as 3
        Yves Veggie Dogs or 2 LightLife Jumbos on buns
    1 cup vegetarian baked beans
    1 cup cooked kale (frozen or fresh)
    2 slices tomato
    1 baked apple made with 1 medium apple, 1/4 cup
        chopped dates, and 1 Tablespoon granulated sweetener
    1 cup Soy Dream Enriched soymilk
Snack:
    1 ounce walnuts
    1/4 cup raisins
    1 bagel
    1 cup Soy Dream Enriched soymilk

Day 6 for Male, 19-50 years old

Breakfast:
>1 cup Wheat Chex cereal or any vegan ready-to-eat cereal with 1 medium peach, sliced, and 1 cup Soy Dream Enriched soymilk
>
>2 slices whole-wheat toast

Lunch:
>1-1/2 sandwiches made with 3 slices whole-wheat bread, 3 Tablespoons nut butter (peanut, almond, cashew, etc.), and 1 Tablespoon jelly
>
>1/3 cup carrot sticks
>
>1 cup grapes
>
>1 cup Soy Dream Enriched soymilk

Dinner:
>1 cup cooked pasta with 1/2 cup kidney beans and 1/2 cup marinara sauce
>
>2 Garden of Eatin' whole-wheat tortillas or any tortillas providing 250-300 calories (for 2 tortillas)
>
>1 medium orange
>
>6 ounces Whole Soy fruited yogurt or any vegan yogurt providing 120-170 calories per serving such as Silk cultured soy fruited yogurt

Snack:
>1 kiwi fruit
>
>1/4 cup soynuts
>
>5 whole-wheat crackers

Day 7 for Male, 19-50 years old

Breakfast:
  1-1/2 cups quick oats with 2 Tablespoons wheat germ
  2 English muffins with 2 teaspoons vegan margarine
  1 cup calcium-fortified apple juice

Lunch:
  Sandwich made with 2 slices whole-wheat bread, 2
    ounces Yves Veggie Bologna Slices or any deli slice
    providing 50-100 calories such as as Lightlife's Smart
    Deli Bologna Style (3 slices), Yves Veggie Salami Slices
    (4 slices), Tofurky Deli Slices (1 ounce), or Vegi-Deli
    Slices (1 ounce), 1 Tablespoon Nayonnaise or any
    vegan spread providing 25-50 calories or can be
    omitted, and 1/2 cup shredded lettuce
  1 wedge watermelon
  1 cup Soy Dream Enriched soymilk

Dinner:
  1/2 cup chickpeas and 3/4 cup peas with 1 Tablespoon
    tahini on 1-1/2 cups couscous
  1 whole-wheat roll
  Smoothie made with 1 cup Soy Dream Enriched soymilk,
    3 ounces soft tofu, 1 medium frozen banana, 1/2 cup
    strawberries, and 1 Tablespoon maple syrup

Snack:
  Hummus made with 1/3 cup chickpeas and 1 teaspoon
    tahini
  1/3 cup carrot sticks
  1 cup celery
  5 whole-wheat crackers

Low-Cost Quick and Easy Vegan Menus for Older People

This second set of menus was devised to meet the needs of men and women age 51 years and older. The menus for men have around 2,300 calories per day while the women's menus are around 1,900 calories. If you are very active, you will need more calories. You have several choices; you can eat more of the foods already on the menus or you can add favorite foods to the menus. Conversely, if you are not very active, you will need fewer calories. In that case, we recommend cutting out some of the "extras" like margarine, chips, desserts, and vegan mayonnaise.

The menus were planned to meet the average person's needs for most nutrients over a week-long period. A vitamin D supplement (5 micrograms for people age 51-70 years old, 10 micrograms for those over age 70) is recommended if your sunlight exposure is limited.

We used specific brand names of foods but have included information on other foods that can be substituted if you don't care for a particular food.

We were curious about how costly these menus would be. The average cost for 1 day's food for a man was a bit over $5.50 using conventional fruits and vegetables and around $7.70 using all organic products. The average cost for one day's food for a woman was around $5.00 using conventional fruits and vegetables and almost $6.40 using all organic products. Pricing was done in the winter in New England so may vary depending on the season, your location, and inflation. If you want to reduce food costs even more, you can buy products when they are on sale, see if your supermarket will offer case discounts for items you use often like soymilk, and choose fruits and vegetables that are in season.

Day 1 for Female, 51+ years old

Breakfast:
- 1/2 cup calcium-fortified orange juice
- 1 medium banana
- 2 slices whole-wheat toast with 1 Tablespoon nut butter (peanut, almond, cashew, etc.)
- 1 cup Wheat Chex cereal or any vegan fortified cereal providing at least 10% of the DV for calcium and 15% of the DV for zinc per cup
- 1 cup Soy Dream Enriched soymilk

Lunch:
- 1 bowl of Fantastic Foods Big Bowl of Noodles and Hot and Sour Soup or any soup/entrée cup providing 250-300 calories/cup, 8 or more grams of protein per cup, and at least 8% of the DV for iron per serving such as Health Valley Lentil with Couscous Soup, Black Bean Chili, Texas-Style Chili, Black Bean with Couscous Soup, Thai Rice, Cantonese Rice, Shiitake Rice, or Pasta Italiano Soup; or Fantastic Foods Jamaican Rice Bowl, Tex-Mex Rice Bowl, Black Bean Salsa Couscous, Country Lentil Soup, Cha-Cha Chili, or 5 Bean Soup
- 10 saltines with 1/2 Tablespoon nut butter (peanut, almond, cashew, etc.)
- 1 medium orange
- 1/2 cup carrot sticks

Dinner:
- 1 Morningstar Farms Harvest Burger or any burger providing at least 140 calories, 18 grams of protein, 8% of the DV for calcium, and 6% of the DV for iron such as 2 Whole Foods Vegan Burgers on a bun with a large slice of tomato
- 1 medium baked potato

Snack:
- 1 cup Soy Dream Enriched soymilk
- 3/4 cup kidney beans mixed with 1 Tablespoon salsa served with 1 ounce lowfat tortilla chips

Day 2 for Female, 51+ years old

Breakfast:
- 1 bagel with 2 teaspoons vegan margarine
- 1 medium orange
- 1 cup Wheat Chex cereal or any vegan fortified cereal providing 10% of the DV for calcium or more per cup
- 1 cup Soy Dream Enriched soymilk

Lunch:
- Hummus sandwich made with 3/4 cup chickpeas and 2 teaspoons tahini on 2 slices of whole-wheat bread with 3 slices of tomato
- 1 medium apple

Dinner:
- 1 cup of cooked pasta with 1/4 cup marinara sauce
- 1/3 cup carrot sticks
- 1 cup cooked broccoli (frozen or fresh)
- 1 whole-wheat roll

Snack:
- 1/4 cup roasted, unsalted soynuts
- 1 cup Soy Dream Enriched soymilk

Note: In all the menus, Soy Dream Enriched soymilk can be replaced with Silk soymilk or any other calcium-fortified soymilk that provides at least 25% of the Daily Value (DV) for vitamin D and 20% of the DV for vitamin B12 in an 8-ounce serving.

Day 3 for Female, 51+ years old

Breakfast:

 Scrambled tofu made with 1/2 cup tofu, 1/4 cup onions, and 1 teaspoon oil

 1/2 cup calcium-fortified orange juice

 2 slices whole-wheat toast

Lunch:

 Sandwich made with 1 large pita bread, 1/2 cup shredded lettuce, 1/4 cup chopped tomato, and 1/4 cup grated carrot

 Fantastic Foods Country Lentil soup cup or any soup cup providing 200-300 calories and 16 or more grams of protein such as Health Valley Chili or Fantastic Foods Cha-Cha Chili

 1 medium banana

 1 cup Soy Dream Enriched soymilk

Dinner:

 1/2 cup kidney beans with 1 cup cooked quick brown rice and 2 Tablespoons salsa

 1 cup frozen mashed squash

Snack:

 1/2 cup trail mix (mix of nuts, raisins, and sunflower seeds)

 1 cup Soy Dream Enriched soymilk

Day 4 for Female, 51+ years old

Breakfast:
>1-1/2 cups cooked quick oats with 3 Tablespoons wheat germ, 1/4 cup raisins, and 1 ounce chopped walnuts
>
>1 cup Soy Dream Enriched soymilk

Lunch:
>Burrito made with 1 Garden of Eatin' whole-wheat tortilla or any tortilla providing 125-150 calories, 1/2 cup black beans, and 1 Tablespoon salsa
>
>1 cup diced cantaloupe

Dinner:
>6 ounces calcium-fortified V-8 juice
>
>Stir-fry made with 1/2 cup diced tofu, 1 cup frozen stir-fry vegetables, 2 Tablespoons soy sauce, 1-1/2 cups cooked quick brown rice, and 1 teaspoon oil

Snack:
>1 cup Soy Dream Enriched soymilk
>
>3 cups popped popcorn with 1 Tablespoon Vegetarian Support Formula nutritional yeast

Don't forget, although these menus provide generous amounts of iron, women may require additional iron in the form of an iron supplement.

Day 5 for Female, 51+ years old

Breakfast:
    1 English muffin with 1 Tablespoon jelly
    1 cup calcium-fortified orange juice
Lunch:
    Baked tofu made with 4 ounces tofu and 1 Tablespoon soy
        sauce
    1 large sweet potato
Dinner:
    2 Yves the Good Dogs or any vegan hot dogs providing
        150-175 calories and 26 or more grams of protein such
        as 3 Yves Veggie Dogs or 2 Lightlife Jumbos
    1 cup vegetarian baked beans
    1-1/2 cups cooked kale (frozen or fresh)
    2 tomato slices
    1 baked apple made with medium apple, 1/4 cup chopped
        dates, and 1 Tablespoon granulated sweetener
    1 cup Soy Dream Enriched soymilk
Snack:
    1 ounce walnuts
    1/4 cup raisins
    1 cup Soy Dream Enriched soymilk

Day 6 for Female, 51+ years old

Breakfast:
>1 cup Wheat Chex cereal or any vegan fortified cereal
>with 1 medium peach, sliced, and 1 cup Soy Dream
>Enriched soymilk
>1 slice whole-wheat toast

Lunch:
>1 sandwich made with 2 slices whole-wheat bread, 2
>Tablespoons nut butter (peanut, almond, cashew, etc.),
>and 1 Tablespoon jelly
>1/3 cup carrot sticks
>1 cup grapes
>1 cup Soy Dream Enriched soymilk

Dinner:
>1/2 cup kidney beans with 1 cup cooked pasta and 1/2 cup
>marinara sauce
>1 Garden of Eatin' whole-wheat tortilla or any tortilla
>providing 125-150 calories
>1 medium orange
>1 cup cooked collard greens (frozen or fresh)

Snack:
>1/4 cup soynuts

Day 7 for Female, 51+ years old

Breakfast:
- 1-1/2 cups cooked quick oats with 2 Tablespoons wheat germ
- 1 English muffin
- 1/2 cup calcium-fortified apple juice

Lunch:
- Sandwich made with 2 slices whole-wheat bread, 2 ounces Yves Veggie Bologna Slices or any deli slice providing 50-100 calories and 12 or more grams of protein per serving such as as Lightlife's Smart Deli Bologna Style (4 slices), Yves Veggie Salami Slices (4 slices), or Vegi-Deli Chicken Style slices (1 ounce), 1/2 cup shredded lettuce, and 2 Slices tomato
- 1 wedge watermelon
- 1 cup Soy Dream Enriched soymilk

Dinner:
- 1/2 cup chickpeas with 1 Tablespoon tahini on 1-1/2 cups cooked couscous
- Smoothie made with 1 cup Soy Dream Enriched soymilk, 3 ounces soft tofu, 1 medium frozen banana, 1/2 cup strawberries, and 1 Tablespoon maple syrup

Snack:
- Hummus made with 1/4 cup chickpeas and 1 teaspoon tahini
- 1/3 cup carrot sticks
- 1/2 cup celery

Day 1 for Male, 51+ years old

Breakfast:
>   1 cup calcium-fortified orange juice
>
>   1 medium banana
>
>   2 slices whole-wheat toast with 1 Tablespoon nut butter
>   (peanut, almond, cashew, etc.)
>
>   1 cup Wheat Chex cereal or any vegan ready-to-eat cereal
>   with at least 25% of the DV for zinc per serving
>
>   1 cup Soy Dream Enriched soymilk

Lunch:
>   1 bowl of Fantastic Foods Big Bowl of Noodles and Hot
>   and Sour Soup or any soup/entrée cup providing 240-300
>   calories/cup and 8 or more grams of protein per cup
>   such as Health Valley Lentil with Couscous Soup or
>   Fantastic Foods Big Bowl of Noodles Spicy Thai,
>   Country Lentil Soup, Cha-Cha Chili, or 5 Bean Soup
>
>   10 saltines with 1 Tablespoon nut butter (peanut, almond,
>   cashew, etc.)
>
>   1 medium orange
>
>   1/2 cup carrot sticks

Dinner:
>   1 Morningstar Farms Harvest Burger or any veggie burger
>   providing at least 140 calories and 18 grams of protein
>   such as 2 Whole Foods Vegan Burgers on a bun with a
>   large slice of tomato
>
>   1 medium baked potato

Snack:
>   1 cup Soy Dream Enriched soymilk
>
>   1 cup of kidney beans mashed with 1 Tablespoon salsa
>
>   1 ounce lowfat tortilla chips

Day 2 for Male, 51+ years old

Breakfast:
 1 bagel
 1 medium orange
 1 cup Wheat Chex cereal or any vegan ready-to-eat cereal
 1 cup Soy Dream Enriched soymilk

Lunch:
 2 hummus sandwiches made with 3/4 cup chickpeas and
   2 teaspoons tahini on 4 slices of whole-wheat bread with
   3 slices of tomato
 1 medium apple

Dinner:
 1 cup cooked pasta with 1/4 cup marinara sauce and
   1/2 cup tofu cubes
 1/3 cup carrot sticks
 1 cup cooked broccoli (frozen or fresh)
 2 whole-wheat rolls
 2 teaspoons vegan margarine

Snack:
 1/3 cup roasted, unsalted soynuts
 1 cup Soy Dream Enriched soymilk

Note: In all the menus, Soy Dream Enriched soymilk can be replaced with Silk soymilk or any other calcium-fortified soymilk that provides at least 25% of the Daily Value (DV) for vitamin D and 20% of the DV for vitamin B12 in an 8-ounce serving.

Day 3 for Male, 51+ years old

Breakfast:
  1 cup calcium-fortified orange juice
  Scrambled tofu made with 1/2 cup tofu, 1/4 cup onions,
    and 2 teaspoons oil
  2 slices whole-wheat toast
Lunch:
  Sandwich made with 1-1/2 large whole-wheat pitas filled
    with 1/2 cup shredded lettuce, 1/4 cup chopped
    tomato, 1/4 cup grated carrots, and 1 Tablespoon
    Nayonnaise or any vegan spread providing 25-50
    calories or can be omitted
  Fantastic Foods Country Lentil soup cup or any soup cup
    providing 200-300 calories and 16 or more grams of
    protein per cup such as Health Valley Chili or Fantastic
    Foods Cha-Cha Chili
  1 medium banana
  1 cup Soy Dream Enriched soymilk
Dinner:
  3/4 cup kidney beans with 1 cup quick brown rice and
    2 Tablespoons salsa
  1 Garden of Eatin' whole-wheat tortilla or any tortilla
    providing 125-150 calories per tortilla
  1 cup frozen mashed squash
  1 cup unsweetened applesauce
Snack:
  1/4 cup roasted, unsalted soynuts
  1 cup Soy Dream Enriched soymilk

Day 4 for Male, 51+ years old

<u>Breakfast</u>:
- 1-1/2 cups quick rolled oats with 2 Tablespoons wheat germ, 1/4 cup chopped dates, and 1 ounce chopped walnuts
- 2 slices whole-wheat toast with 1 Tablespoon nut butter (peanut, almond, cashew, etc.)
- 1 cup Soy Dream Enriched soymilk

<u>Lunch</u>:
- Burrito made with 1 Garden of Eatin' whole-wheat tortilla or any tortilla providing 125-150 calories per tortilla, 1/2 cup black beans, and 1 Tablespoon salsa
- 1 ounce lowfat tortilla chips
- 1/4 cup salsa
- 1 medium apple

<u>Dinner</u>:
- Stir-fry made with 3/4 cup tofu cubes, 1 cup frozen stir-fry vegetables, 2 Tablespoons soy sauce, 1 teaspoon oil, and 1-1/2 cups cooked quick brown rice
- 1 cup diced cantaloupe

<u>Snack</u>:
- 1 cup Soy Dream Enriched soymilk
- 3 cups popped popcorn sprinkled with 1 Tablespoon Vegetarian Support Formula nutritional yeast

Day 5 for Male, 51+ years old

Breakfast:
>1 English muffin with 1/2 Tablespoon jelly
>1 cup grape juice

Lunch:
>Baked tofu made with 4 ounces sliced tofu and 1 Tablespoon soy sauce
>1 large sweet potato
>1 ounce walnuts
>1/4 cup raisins

Dinner:
>2 Yves the Good Dogs or any vegan hot dogs providing 150-175 calories and 26 or more grams of protein such as 3 Yves Veggie Dogs or 2 Lightlife Jumbos on buns
>1 cup vegetarian baked beans
>1 cup cooked kale (frozen or fresh)
>2 slices tomato
>1 baked apple made with medium apple, 1/4 cup chopped dates, and 1 Tablespoon granulated sweetener
>1 cup Soy Dream Enriched soymilk

Snack:
>1 bagel
>1 cup Soy Dream Enriched soymilk

Day 6 for Male, 51+ years old

Breakfast:
- 1 cup Wheat Chex cereal or any vegan ready-to-eat cereal with 1 medium peach, sliced, and 1 cup Soy Dream Enriched soymilk
- 2 slices whole-wheat toast

Lunch:
- 1-1/2 sandwiches made with 3 slices whole-wheat bread, 3 Tablespoons nut butter (peanut, almond, cashew, etc.), and 1 Tablespoon jelly
- 1/3 cup carrot sticks
- 1 cup grapes
- 1 cup Soy Dream Enriched soymilk

Dinner:
- 1 cup cooked pasta with 1/2 cup kidney beans and 1/2 cup marinara sauce
- 1 Garden of Eatin' whole-wheat tortilla or any tortillas providing 125-150 calories per tortilla
- 1 medium orange
- 6 ounces Whole Soy fruited yogurt or any vegan yogurt providing 120-170 calories and 4 or more grams of protein per serving such as White Wave Silk Cultured Soy

Snack:
- 1/4 cup soynuts
- 1/2 cup Soy Dream Enriched soymilk

Day 7 for Male, 51+ years old

Breakfast:
  1-1/2 cups quick oats with 2 Tablespoons wheat germ
  2 English muffins
  1/2 cup calcium-fortified apple juice

Lunch:
  Sandwich made with 2 slices whole-wheat bread, 2
    ounces Yves Veggie Bologna Slices or any deli slice
    providing 50-100 calories and 12 or more grams of
    protein per serving such as Lightlife's Smart Deli
    Bologna Style (4 slices), Yves Veggie Salami Slices
    (4 slices), or Vegi-Deli Chicken Style Slices (1 ounce),
    1 Tablespoon Nayonnaise or any vegan spread pro-
    viding 25-50 calories or can be omitted, and 1/2 cup
    shredded lettuce
  1 wedge watermelon
  1 cup Soy Dream Enriched soymilk

Dinner:
  1/2 cup chickpeas and 3/4 cup peas with 1 Tablespoon
    tahini on 1-1/2 cups couscous
  1 whole-wheat roll
  Smoothie made with 1 cup Soy Dream Enriched soymilk,
    3 ounces soft tofu, 1 medium frozen banana, 1/2 cup
    strawberries, and 1 Tablespoon maple syrup

Snack:
  Hummus made with 1/3 cup chickpeas and 1 teaspoon
    tahini
  1/3 cup carrot sticks
  1 cup celery

RECIPES

The toughest barriers to quick and easy vegetarian cooking are the habits we have developed throughout our lifetime. Once you break that mental resistance, ideas for meals will come to you naturally, meal preparation will become routine and go much faster.

This section has some ideas to get you started. You may want to adjust the amount of spices to your taste. Eliminate salt and soy sauce or tamari and use low sodium tomato sauce and tomato paste if you are on a low sodium diet. If you are on a lowfat diet, when a recipe calls for oil for sautéing vegetables, use slightly more water or vegetable broth instead of the oil.

Recipes were analyzed using Nutritionist IV and manufacturer's information. Optional ingredients were omitted. If ingredient choices were listed (i.e. green or red cabbage), the first ingredient was used in analysis. If a range of servings was specified (i.e. 4-6), the lowest number of servings was used for analysis.

Breakfast Ideas

BROILED GRAPEFRUIT
(Serves 4)

2 large grapefruits, sliced in half, seeds removed
2 Tablespoons maple syrup
1/2 teaspoon cinnamon

Loosen grapefruit sections with a knife. Place grapefruit halves fruit side up on a baking pan and spread 1/2 Tablespoon maple syrup on each half. Sprinkle 1/8 teaspoon cinnamon on each grapefruit half and place under a broiler for 7 minutes. Serve warm.

Total calories per serving: 98
Fat: <1 gram   Total Fat as % of Daily Value: <1%
Protein: 2 grams   Iron: 1 mg   Carbohydrate: 24 grams
Calcium: 81 mg   Dietary fiber: 11 grams

APPLESAUCE
(Serves 6)

6 apples, diced finely
1 Tablespoon cinnamon
1 teaspoon nutmeg
2 oranges, peeled and sliced
Water

Put about 1/3-inch of water in a large pot. Add all the ingredients and cook over medium heat until the apples are soft, stirring occasionally. For variety you can add 1/4 cup raisins.

Total calories per serving: 103
Fat: 2 grams   Total Fat as % of Daily Value: 2%
Protein: 1 gram   Iron: <1 mg   Carbohydrate: 26 grams
Calcium: 27 mg   Dietary fiber: 4 grams

OATMEAL/APPLES/RAISINS AND CINNAMON
(Serves 4)

1 cup rolled oats
3 cups water
2 apples, chopped
1/2 cup raisins
1 teaspoon cinnamon

Heat the above ingredients together in a pot over medium heat for about 5 minutes until oats are cooked. Stir occasionally to prevent sticking.

Total calories per serving: 173
Fat: 2 grams   Total Fat as % of Daily Value: 3%
Protein: 4 grams   Iron: 1 mg   Carbohydrate: 38 grams
Calcium: 24 mg   Dietary fiber: 3 grams

CORNMEAL MUSH
(Serves 2)

1/2 cup quick cooking cornmeal
1-1/2 cups water
1/2 cup chopped fresh fruit (blueberries, bananas, straw-
   berries, etc.)

Cook cornmeal in water according to directions on the box, adding chopped fruit just before serving.

Total calories per serving: 163
Fat: 1 gram   Total Fat as % of Daily Value: 2%
Protein: 3 grams   Iron: 2 mg   Carbohydrate: 36 grams
Calcium: 5 mg   Dietary fiber: 3 grams

CINNAMON/SLICED APPLE TOAST
(Serves 6)

6 slices whole wheat bread or English muffins
2-3 apples, thinly sliced
1 Tablespoon brown sugar (optional)
1 Tablespoon vegan margarine
1/2 teaspoon cinnamon

Toast bread. Place several slices of apple, dots of margarine, sprinkle of brown sugar, and a dash of cinnamon on toast or muffin. Place under a broiler until the margarine melts.

Total calories per serving: 114
Fat: 3 grams   Total Fat as % of Daily Value: 5%
Protein: 3 grams   Iron: 1 mg   Carbohydrate: 20 grams
Calcium: 24 mg   Dietary fiber: 1 gram

CORNBREAD AND BLUEBERRIES
(Serves 6)

8-ounce box vegan cornbread mix (Beware: some mixes contain lard!)
1 cup blueberries

Preheat oven to 350 degrees. Add blueberries to batter prepared from a cornbread mix. Pour into lightly oiled 9-inch square cake pan. Bake until done at 350 degrees (approximately 15 minutes).

Total calories per serving: 161
Fat: 4 grams   Total Fat as % of Daily Value: 6%
Protein: 3 grams   Iron: 1 mg   Carbohydrate: 30 grams
Calcium: 1 mg   Dietary fiber: 1 gram

EGGLESS BANANA PANCAKES
(Serves 2)

1/2 cup rolled oats
1/2 cup whole wheat pastry flour or unbleached white flour
1/2 cup cornmeal (white or yellow)
1 Tablespoon baking powder
1-1/2 cups water
2 large ripe bananas, sliced or mashed
2 teaspoons oil

Mix all the ingredients together in a bowl. Use about 1/4 cup of batter per pancake, poured into lightly oiled preheated frying pan. Fry over low heat on one side until light brown, then flip over and fry on the other side until done.

Variations: Add chopped apples, raisins, or blueberries to the batter before frying.

Total calories per serving: 482
Fat: 8 grams   Total Fat as % of Daily Value: 12%
Protein: 12 grams   Iron: 4 mg   Carbohydrate: 97 grams
Calcium: 306 mg   Dietary fiber: 9 grams

EGGLESS FRENCH TOAST
(Serves 3-4)

3 ripe bananas
1 cup soy or rice milk
2 Tablespoons molasses or maple syrup
1/4 teaspoon cinnamon
7 slices whole wheat bread
2 teaspoons oil

Mash bananas in a bowl. Add soy or rice milk, molasses or maple syrup, and cinnamon. Stir well.
     Soak bread in above mixture. Fry in lightly oiled frying pan on both sides over medium heat until lightly brown.

Total calories per serving: 380
Fat: 9 grams   Total Fat as % of Daily Value: 14%
Protein: 10 grams   Iron: 4 mg   Carbohydrate: 70 grams
Calcium: 121 mg   Dietary fiber: 2 grams

HASH BROWN POTATOES
(Serves 4)

2 teaspoons oil
4 large white potatoes, cleaned and thinly sliced
1 large onion, chopped
1/2 teaspoon garlic powder
1/4 teaspoon paprika
Salt and pepper to taste

Heat oil in a frying pan over a medium-high heat. Add potatoes
and onion. Add seasonings and stir-fry until potatoes are soft
(about 15 minutes).

Total calories per serving: 307
Fat: 3 grams   Total Fat as % of Daily Value: 5%
Protein: 6 grams   Iron: 4 mg   Carbohydrate: 66 grams
Calcium: 31 mg   Dietary fiber: 7 grams

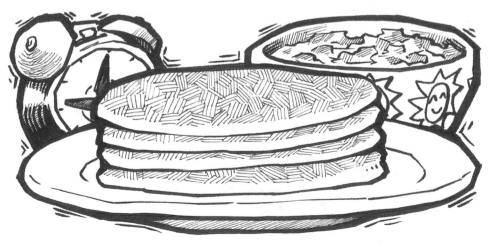

Beverages

HOT APPLE CIDER
(Serves 8)

1/2 gallon apple cider
1 lemon, sliced thinly
1-1/2 teaspoons cinnamon
1/4 teaspoon nutmeg

Heat all the above ingredients in a large pot over medium heat, stirring occasionally, until heated through. Serve warm in mugs.

Total calories per serving: 127
Fat: <1 gram   Total Fat as % of Daily Value: <1%
Protein: <1 grams   Iron: 1 mg   Carbohydrate: 36 grams
Calcium: 23 mg   Dietary fiber: <1 grams

BLENDED FRUIT DRINK
(Serves 4)

3 ripe bananas, sliced
6 strawberries
4 cups chilled orange juice

Blend all the ingredients above in a blender and serve.

Variations: Use different fruit juices and or other fruits such as peaches and apples.

Total calories per serving: 195
Fat: 1 gram   Total Fat as % of Daily Value: 2%
Protein: 3 grams   Iron: 1 mg   Carbohydrate: 48 grams
Calcium: 29 mg   Dietary fiber: 2 grams

QUICK CASHEW MILK
(Serves 4)

1 cup raw cashews
3 cups water

Blend the cashews and water in a blender for 5 minutes and refrigerate. Use as a beverage or in recipes calling for milk. Shake well before serving.

Total calories per serving: 196
Fat: 16 grams   Total Fat as % of Daily Value: 25%
Protein: 5 grams   Iron: 2 mg   Carbohydrate: 11 grams
Calcium: 16 mg   Dietary fiber: 2 grams

EASY ALMOND NUT MILK
(Serves 2)

1/2 cup almonds
1-1/2 cups boiling water

Blend almonds and boiling water in a blender for about 3 minutes at a high speed. Strain through muslin or cheesecloth. (The remaining pulp can be used in burgers or vegetable/nut loaves.) Shake milk well before serving.

Total calories per serving: 172
Fat: 15 grams   Total Fat as % of Daily Value: 24%
Protein: 8 grams   Iron: 2 mg   Carbohydrate: 6 grams
Calcium: 114 mg   Dietary fiber: 3 grams

MILK SHAKE
(Serves 3)

3 cups chilled nut milk (see above recipes)
6 Tablespoons cocoa or carob powder
2/3 cup shredded coconut
Sweetener to taste (maple syrup, etc.)

Blend above ingredients together in a blender at a high speed for 2 minutes. Serve immediately.

Total calories per serving (using cashew milk): 373
Fat: 24 grams   Total Fat as % of Daily Value: 37%
Protein: 8 grams   Iron: 4 mg   Carbohydrate: 35 grams
Calcium: 32 mg   Dietary fiber: 5 grams

SPARKLING SELTZER
(Serves 1)

8 ounces seltzer (salt-free)
2 Tablespoons frozen juice concentrate (orange, grapefruit,
    lemon, grape, etc.)

Pour chilled seltzer into a glass. Add frozen juice concentrate. Stir well, and enjoy!

Variation: Add ½ cup juice instead of frozen concentrate to ½ cup seltzer.

Total calories per serving (using orange juice concentrate): 56
Fat: <1 grams   Total Fat as % of Daily Value: <1%
Protein: 1 grams   Iron: <1 mg   Carbohydrate: 14 grams
Calcium: 19 mg   Dietary fiber: <1 grams

Salads and Dressings

COLESLAW
(Serves 4)

1/2 medium head green cabbage, shredded
4 carrots, grated
1/2 cup lemon juice
1/2 cup eggless mayonnaise (found in natural foods stores)

Mix all the ingredients together in a large bowl. Chill and toss before serving.

Variations: Add grated apples, crushed pineapple, raisins, and/ or toasted sunflower seeds.

Total calories per serving: 129
Fat: 6 grams   Total Fat as % of Daily Value: 9%
Protein: 2 grams   Iron: 1 mg   Carbohydrate: 16 grams
Calcium: 65 mg   Dietary fiber: 3 grams

A HEFTY SALAD
(Serves 4)

1 stalk celery, diced
1 large carrot, grated
1 clove garlic, minced (optional)
1/2 cup toasted sunflower or pumpkin seeds
2 Tablespoons eggless mayonnaise or dressing of choice
Salt and pepper to taste
1/2 pound lettuce or raw spinach leaves

Mix ingredients (except lettuce or spinach leaves) well in a large bowl and serve on ½ pound lettuce or raw spinach leaves.

Total calories per serving (including lettuce): 139
Fat: 11 grams   Total Fat as % of Daily Value: 17%
Protein: 5 grams   Iron: 2 mg   Carbohydrate: 8 grams
Calcium: 42 mg   Dietary fiber: 3 gram

STUFFED TOMATO SALAD
(Serves 5)

5 large ripe tomatoes
**8-ounce can chickpeas (or about 1 cup precooked chick-
    peas)**
1 stalk celery, chopped (optional)
Salt and pepper to taste

Scoop out tomatoes, saving pulp to use as a sauce. Fill tomatoes
with chickpeas and celery.   Season with salt and pepper.
Garnish with sauce and lettuce or sprouts.

Total calories per serving: 80
Fat: 2 grams   Total Fat as % of Daily Value: 3%
Protein: 3 grams   Iron: 1 mg   Carbohydrate: 15 grams
Calcium: 24 mg   Dietary fiber: 5 grams

CUCUMBER SALAD
(Serves 6)

3 cucumbers, sliced
1/2 cup white vinegar
1 small onion, minced
Pepper to taste

Mix all the ingredients together in a bowl. Serve immediately;
however, the salad tastes better if allowed to sit in the
refrigerator for a day or two. Store in a jar.

Total calories per serving: 26
Fat: <1 gram   Total Fat as % of Daily Value: <1%
Protein: 1 grams   Iron: 1 mg   Carbohydrate: 6 grams
Calcium: 25 mg   Dietary fiber: <1 gram

BEET SALAD
(Serves 4)

2 large beets, grated
1/2 medium head cabbage, shredded
3 carrots, grated
Handful of raisins
1 apple, diced
1/4 cup lemon juice
1/4 cup oil
1/4 cup water

Toss all the ingredients together in a large bowl and mix well.

Variations: Use raw sweet potato instead of beets. Add sunflower seeds, crushed pineapple, or other fruit.

Total calories per serving: 232
Fat: 14 grams   Total Fat as % of Daily Value: 21%
Protein: 3 grams   Iron: 1 mg   Carbohydrate: 27 grams
Calcium: 71 mg   Dietary fiber: 4 grams

SUMMER FRUIT SALAD
(Serves 12)

Large fresh pineapple
6 large pieces other fruit (i.e. apples, peaches, plums, etc.)
3 Tablespoons shredded coconut

Stand pineapple upright and cut it in half vertically. Carve out pineapple into bite size pieces. Cut up additional fruit into small pieces. Mix all the fruit together and pour back into pineapple shell. Sprinkle with shredded coconut and serve chilled.

Total calories per serving (using apples, peaches, and plums): 65
Fat: 1 gram   Total Fat as % of Daily Value: 2%
Protein: 1 gram   Iron: <1 mg   Carbohydrate: 15 grams
Calcium: 7 mg   Dietary fiber: 2 grams

POTATO SALAD AND OLIVES
(Serves 4)

4 large white potatoes, peeled and cubed into small pieces
Water
10-ounce box frozen mixed vegetables
1 small onion, chopped finely
1/3 cup black olives, drained and sliced
1 teaspoon celery seed
Salt and pepper to taste
1/2 cup eggless mayonnaise

Cover potatoes with water in a large pot and cook until tender over medium heat. Drain potatoes. At the same time, cook mixed vegetables in a separate pot until tender. Drain vegetables. Mix the ingredients together in a large bowl. Season and add mayonnaise according to your taste.

Variations: Instead of frozen vegetables, add raw vegetables such as finely chopped celery and/or carrots. Add finely chopped parsley. You may also want to use canned pre-cooked Irish potatoes to save more time.

Total calories per serving: 348
Fat: 12 grams   Total Fat as % of Daily Value: 18%
Protein: 9 grams   Iron: 4 mg   Carbohydrate: 55 grams
Calcium: 80 mg   Dietary fiber: 8 grams

MACARONI SALAD
(Serves 6)

3 cups pre-cooked macaroni
2 stalks celery, diced
1 carrot, diced
1 cup peas (frozen or fresh), cooked
1 small onion, finely chopped
Eggless mayonnaise to taste
Salt and pepper to taste

Mix all the ingredients together in a large bowl.

Variations: Add sliced pickles, other vegetables, or olives.

Total calories per serving (using ½ cup mayonnaise): 152
Fat: 4 grams   Total Fat as % of Daily Value: 6%
Protein: 4 grams   Iron: 1 mg   Carbohydrate: 6 grams
Calcium: 9 mg   Dietary fiber: 2 grams

TOMATO SALAD
(Serves 4)

4 tomatoes, cut into 1/2-inch wedges
2 Tablespoons oil
1/4 cup water
1 teaspoon lemon juice
2 cloves garlic, minced
Oregano and salt to taste

Mix all the ingredients together in a bowl and serve.

Total calories per serving: 89
Fat: grams   Total Fat as % of Daily Value: 11%
Protein: 1 gram   Iron: 1 mg   Carbohydrate: 6 grams
Calcium: 9 mg   Dietary fiber: 2 grams

CRANBERRY SALAD
(Serves 12)

12 ounces fresh or frozen cranberries
1/2 cup orange juice or apple juice
1 cup raisins
1 cup shredded coconut
2 stalks celery, chopped finely
1 apple, chopped finely
1/4 cup chopped walnuts (optional)

Blend cranberries, juice, and raisins together in a blender. Pour in to a large bowl and add coconut, celery, apple, and walnuts if desired. Toss well before serving.

Total calories per serving: 102
Fat: 3 grams   Total Fat as % of Daily Value: 5%
Protein: 1 gram   Iron: 1 mg   Carbohydrate: 20 grams
Calcium: 14 mg   Dietary fiber: 2 grams

SWEET RAINBOW DELIGHT
(Serves 6)

3 apples, grated
3 carrots, grated
1/3 cup shredded coconut
1/2 cup raisins

Toss all the ingredients together in a bowl and serve.

Variation: Add chopped dates instead of raisins.

Total calories per serving: 116
Fat: 2 grams   Total Fat as % of Daily Value: 26%
Protein: 1 gram   Iron: 1 mg   Carbohydrate: 26 grams
Calcium: 21 mg   Dietary fiber: 3 grams

RAW VEGETABLE PLATTER
(Serves 12)

Chop up into bite-size pieces 3 to 4 pounds of vegetables including: celery, carrots, broccoli, tomatoes, squash, and mushrooms. Arrange on a large platter. Serve with your favorite dips and spreads or the dressings below.

Nutritional breakdown will vary depending upon vegetables and dressings selected.

SWEET FRENCH DRESSING
(Makes 2 cups)

1 cup oil
2 oranges, peeled and seeds taken out
2 Tablespoons lemon juice
1 Tablespoon white vinegar
1 teaspoon paprika
1 teaspoon salt
Slice of onion, minced

Blend all the ingredients together in a blender for 3 minutes and serve over your favorite salad or raw vegetables.

Total calories per 2 Tablespoon serving: 129
Fat: 14 grams   Total Fat as % of Daily Value: 22%
Protein: <1 gram   Iron: <1 mg   Carbohydrate: 2 grams
Calcium: 7 mg   Dietary fiber: <1 gram

LEMON/APPLE/GARLIC DRESSING
(Makes 3 cups)

1 cup white vinegar
1-1/2 cups water
2 Tablespoons lemon juice
2 cloves garlic, minced
1/4 teaspoon pepper
1/4 teaspoon salt
1 apple — peeled, cored and chopped

Blend all the ingredients together in a blender for 3 minutes.

Total calories per 2 Tablespoon serving: 5
Fat: <1 grams   Total Fat as % of Daily Value: <1%
Protein: <1 gram   Iron: <1 mg   Carbohydrate: 2 grams
Calcium: 2 mg   Dietary fiber: <1 gram

RED BEET DRESSING
(Makes 2 cups)

1 beet, peeled and chopped
1 cup orange juice
1/2 cup oil
1 clove garlic, minced
Salt and pepper to taste

Blend all the ingredients together in a blender for 3 minutes.

Total calories per 2 Tablespoon serving: 69
Fat: 7 grams   Total Fat as % of Daily Value: 11%
Protein: <1 gram   Iron: <1 mg   Carbohydrate: 2 grams
Calcium: 2 mg   Dietary fiber: <1 gram

Soups

VEGETABLE RICE SOUP
(Serves 6-8)

1 cup white rice
6 cups water
1/2 cup parsley, chopped
10-ounce box frozen mixed vegetables
1 medium onion, chopped
Pepper and salt to taste

Cook all the ingredients in a large pot over medium heat until rice is tender (about 30 minutes).

Total calories per serving: 153
Fat: <1 gram   Total Fat as % of Daily Value: <1%
Protein: 4 grams   Iron: 2 mg   Carbohydrate: 34 grams
Calcium: 25 mg   Dietary fiber: 2 grams

FRESH TOMATO SOUP
(Serves 4)

1 large onion, chopped
5 small ripe tomatoes, chopped
1-1/2 cups water
1 teaspoon dried parsley flakes or 2 teaspoons fresh parsley, minced
Dash of pepper and salt

Combine ingredients in a large pot. Cook over medium heat for 15 minutes. Cool a few minutes; then blend in a blender, reheat, and serve warm.

Total calories per serving: 36
Fat: <1 gram   Total Fat as % of Daily Value: <1%
Protein: 1 gram   Iron: 1 mg   Carbohydrate: 8 grams
Calcium: 12 mg   Dietary fiber: 2 grams

CREAMED CARROT SOUP
(Serves 6)

1 pound carrots, chopped
1 large onion, chopped
1-1/2 Tablespoons oil
6 cups water
1/2 teaspoon salt
1/3 cup fresh parsley, finely chopped

Sauté the chopped onions and carrots in oil for 5 minutes in a large pot. Add water, salt, and parsley. Bring to a boil. Reduce heat, cover, and simmer for 20 more minutes. Puree mixture in a blender and reheat.

Total calories per serving: 72
Fat: 4 grams   Total Fat as % of Daily Value: 6%
Protein: 1 gram   Iron: 1 mg   Carbohydrate: 10 grams
Calcium: 29 mg   Dietary fiber: 2 grams

CREAM OF BROCCOLI SOUP
(Serves 8)

1 pound broccoli, chopped
1/2 pound mushrooms, chopped
1 small onion, chopped
1 teaspoon tarragon
3 cups soy and/or rice milk
Salt and pepper to taste

Steam vegetables and onion together for 10 minutes. Blend half of the steamed vegetables in a blender or food processor along with 1-1/2 cups soy and/or rice milk. Pour into a large pot. Blend remaining steamed vegetables and soy and/or rice milk. Add to pot. Season with tarragon, salt, and pepper, and reheat for 5 minutes over medium heat. Add water if you prefer thinner soup. Serve warm.

Total calories per serving: 86
Fat: 3 grams   Total Fat as % of Daily Value: 5%
Protein: 6 grams   Iron: 1 mg   Carbohydrate: 10 grams
Calcium: 60 mg   Dietary fiber: 3 grams

CREAMED ZUCCHINI/POTATO SOUP
(Serves 6)

1 small onion, chopped
3 Tablespoons oil
3 or 4 medium zucchini, chopped
2 large white potatoes, scrubbed and cut into small cubes
6 cups water
1/2 cup rolled oats
1/2 teaspoon salt
2 Tablespoons fresh parsley, finely chopped

Sauté onion in oil in a large pot for 2 minutes. Add chopped zucchini and cubed potatoes. Sauté for 5 minutes longer. Add water, oats, and seasoning. Simmer for 15 minutes. Puree mixture in a blender, reheat, and serve warm.

Total calories per serving: 168
Fat: 8 grams   Total Fat as % of Daily Value: 12%
Protein: 4 grams   Iron: 2 mg   Carbohydrate: 23 grams
Calcium: 35 mg   Dietary fiber: 3 grams

Lunch Ideas

MOCK "TUNA" SALAD
(Serves 3)

1 cup chickpeas (canned or pre-cooked and drained)
1 stalk celery
1/2 small onion, finely chopped
3 Tablespoons eggless mayonnaise
Salt and pepper to taste

Mash the chickpeas in a small bowl. Add remaining ingredients and mix well. Spread on whole grain bread as a sandwich or serve on a bed of lettuce.

Total calories per serving: 122
Fat: 5 grams Total Fat as % of Daily Value: 8%
Protein: 4 grams   Iron: 1 mg   Carbohydrate: 17 grams
Calcium: 35 mg   Dietary fiber: 5 grams

SPINACH/MUSHROOM SANDWICH
(Serves 6)

10-ounce box frozen spinach
1 cup mushrooms, sliced finely
1 pint sour cream (look for non-dairy sour cream found in
    natural food stores and kosher supermarkets)
6 thick slices whole grain bread or English muffins

Cook spinach per instruction on box and drain well. Place cooked spinach and sliced mushrooms on the bread. Cover with sour cream. Place in toaster oven under low heat until hot. Serve warm.

Total calories per serving: 184
Fat: 9 grams   Total Fat as % of Daily Value: 14%
Protein: 7 grams   Iron: 2 mg   Carbohydrate: 22 grams
Calcium: 354 mg   Dietary fiber: 4 grams

QUICK PIZZA
(Serves 6)

3 English muffins or 6 slices whole wheat bread
1 cup tomato sauce
6 slices vegan cheese
Italian seasoning to taste
1/2 cup chopped vegetables (i.e. sliced onion, chopped
   green peppers, sliced mushrooms, and/or sliced olives)

Toast the English muffin or bread. Spoon sauce over top of
bread. Lay slices of cheese on top. Season to taste. Put on
optional toppings and place pizza in a toaster oven until the
cheese melts (approximately 5-10 minutes). Serve warm.

Total calories per serving: 128
Fat: 3 grams   Total Fat as % of Daily Value: 5%
Protein: 4 grams   Iron: 1 mg   Carbohydrate: 20 grams
Calcium: 244 mg   Dietary fiber: 1 gram

POTATO PANCAKES
(Serves 6)

3 cups cooked white potatoes, mashed
1 small onion, chopped
Salt and pepper to taste
1/4 cup fresh parsley, finely chopped (optional)
2 Tablespoons oil

Mix the mashed potatoes, onion, and seasonings together. Heat oil in a large frying pan. Pour pancakes onto heated pan and fry on each side until light brown (about 8 minutes per side). Serve warm alone or with applesauce.

Total calories per serving: 113
Fat: 5 grams   Total Fat as % of Daily Value: 8%
Protein: 2 grams   Iron: <1 mg   Carbohydrate: 17 grams
Calcium: 6 mg   Dietary fiber: 1 gram

CORN FRITTERS
(Serves 6)

2 cups corn kernels (fresh, frozen, or canned and drained)
1 cup flour
1-1/2 Tablespoons corn starch
1-1/4 cups water
1 Tablespoon oil

Mix all the ingredients (except oil) in a medium-size bowl. Pour batter into a lightly oiled frying pan over medium heat and fry for 3-5 minutes. Turn fritters over and continue frying for 3 minutes longer. Serve warm.

Variations: Instead of corn use other chopped vegetables.

Total calories per serving: 157
Fat: 3 grams   Total Fat as % of Daily Value: 5%
Protein: 4 grams   Iron: 1 mg   Carbohydrate: 18 grams
Calcium: 3 mg   Dietary fiber: 2 grams

COUSCOUS/SQUASH BURGERS
(Makes 12 — serve 2 burgers per person)

3 cups cooked couscous (about ¾ of 10-ounce box)
1-1/2 pounds grated zucchini and/or yellow squash
1/2 small onion, finely chopped
1/2 cup unbleached white flour
2-1/2 teaspoons marjoram
Salt and pepper to taste
1 Tablespoon oil

Mix all the ingredients (except oil) together. Using wet hands, form 12 flat burgers. Fry for 10 minutes on each side in a lightly oiled frying pan over medium-high heat. Serve warm alone or on whole wheat buns for sandwiches.

Total calories per serving: 176
Fat: 3 grams   Total Fat as % of Daily Value: 5%
Protein: 6 grams   Iron: 1 mg   Carbohydrate: 33 grams
Calcium: 27 mg   Dietary fiber: 6 grams

RICE BURGERS
(Makes 6 burgers)

2 cups rice, cooked (leftover cooked rice is great)
1/2 cup bread crumbs
1 cup mixed vegetables (i.e. celery, carrots, squash,
   broccoli), finely chopped
Salt and pepper to taste
1/3 cup oil

Mix rice, bread crumbs, vegetables, and seasonings together. Using wet hands, form 6 flat burgers. Fry for 8-10 minutes on each side in a lightly oiled frying pan over medium-high heat. Serve warm alone or on whole wheat buns with lettuce for sandwiches.

Variations: Instead of cooked rice, use cooked barley. Also, add a small onion, finely chopped.

Total calories per burger (using celery, carrots, squash, and broccoli): 223
Fat: 13 grams   Total Fat as % of Daily Value: 20%
Protein: 3 grams   Iron: 1 mg   Carbohydrate: 25 grams
Calcium: 18 mg   Dietary fiber: 1 gram

LENTIL BURGERS
(Makes 6)

1 cup lentils, pre-cooked in 2-1/2 cups water and drained
1 small onion, finely chopped
1/2 cup wheat germ
1/2 teaspoon garlic powder
Salt and pepper to taste
1 Tablespoon oil

Mix all the ingredients together. Using wet hands, form 6 patties. Fry for 10 minutes on each side in a lightly oiled frying pan over medium heat. Serve warm alone or on a roll with lettuce and tomato.

Total calories per burger: 147
Fat: 4 grams   Total Fat as % of Daily Value: 6%
Protein: 10 grams   Iron: 3 mg   Carbohydrate: 21 grams
Calcium: 21 mg   Dietary fiber: 4 grams

Side Dishes

CAULIFLOWER AU GRATIN
(Serves 4)

10-ounce box frozen cauliflower
1-1/2 cups bread crumbs
2 teaspoons oil
4 slices vegan cheese, cut into strips
Salt and pepper to taste

Cook cauliflower according to directions on the box and drain. Preheat oven to 350 degrees. Roll cooked cauliflower in bread crumbs and place in oiled baking dish. Add strips of cheese and seasoning. Bake at 350 degrees until cheese melts.

Total calories per serving: 225
Fat: 7 grams   Total Fat as % of Daily Value: 11%
Protein: 8 grams   Iron: 2 mg   Carbohydrate: 34 grams
Calcium: 245 mg   Dietary fiber: 3 grams

SCALLOPED CORN AND TOMATOES
(Serves 6)

2 Teaspoons oil
4 large tomatoes, sliced thickly
15-ounce can corn kernels, drained or 10-ounce box frozen
    corn kernels
1 cup bread crumbs
2 Tablespoons margarine

Preheat oven to 350 degrees. Spread oil in an approximately 8-inch x 2-inch tall round baking dish. Place tomatoes on the bottom and mix in the corn. Top with bread crumbs and dot with margarine. Bake at 350 degrees about 20 minutes or until crumbs are toasted. Serve warm.

Total calories per serving: 201
Fat: 7 grams   Total Fat as % of Daily Value: 11%
Protein: 6 grams   Iron: 1 mg   Carbohydrate: 18 grams
Calcium: 27 mg   Dietary fiber: 4 grams

LEFTOVER POTATO DISH
(Serves 6)

2 Tablespoons oil
2 cups leftover baked or boiled potatoes, sliced
1 large onion, chopped
1 cup leftover cooked vegetables
Paprika, garlic powder, salt, and pepper to taste

Heat oil in a large frying pan over medium-high heat. Fry potatoes and onions for 5 minutes. Add vegetables and seasonings and continue heating for 5 more minutes. Serve warm.

Total calories per serving (using broccoli and carrots): 114
Fat: 5 grams   Total Fat as % of Daily Value: 8%
Protein: 2 grams   Iron: 1 mg   Carbohydrate: 17 grams
Calcium: 21 mg   Dietary fiber: 2 grams

GREEN BEANS WITH HERB SAUCE
(Serves 4)

10-ounce box frozen French-style green beans
1/2 small onion, finely chopped
2 Tablespoons vegan margarine
1 Tablespoon fresh parsley, finely chopped
1/4 teaspoon thyme
1-1/2 Tablespoons lemon juice
Paprika, salt, and pepper to taste

Cook green beans per directions on box and drain. Place cooked green beans in a serving dish. Sauté onion in margarine in a medium-size frying pan over medium heat for 3 minutes. Add remaining ingredients and mix well. Once heated pour over cooked green beans and serve.

Total calories per serving: 72
Fat: 6 grams   Total Fat as % of Daily Value: 9%
Protein: 1 gram   Iron: 1 mg   Carbohydrate: 6 grams
Calcium: 38 mg   Dietary fiber: 1 gram

SAUTÉED MUSHROOMS
(Serves 4)

2 Tablespoons vegan margarine or oil
1 pound mushrooms, cleaned and chopped
1 large onion, finely chopped
Garlic powder, salt, and pepper to taste

Heat margarine or oil in a large frying pan over medium-high heat. Sauté mushrooms and onion for 5 minutes. Season to taste and cook over low heat for 3 minutes longer or until mushrooms are tender. Serve warm.

Total calories per serving: 89
Fat: 6 grams   Total Fat as % of Daily Value: 9%
Protein: 3 grams   Iron: 1 mg   Carbohydrate: 8 grams
Calcium: 14 mg   Dietary fiber: 2 grams

CABBAGE DISH
(Serves 6)

1 Tablespoon oil
1 medium-size head green cabbage, shredded
1/2 cup toasted sesame seeds
6 slices vegan cheese

Sauté cabbage and sesame seeds in oil in a large frying pan over medium-high heat until cabbage is tender. Add strips of cheese and cook over low heat until cheese melts. Serve warm.

Variation: Use lettuce, spinach, or bok choy instead of cabbage.

Total calories per serving: 162
Fat: 10 grams   Total Fat as % of Daily Value: 15%
Protein: 5 grams   Iron: 2 mg   Carbohydrate: 13 grams
Calcium: 362 mg   Dietary fiber: 4 grams

SPANISH RICE
(Serves 3)

1 medium onion, finely chopped
1 large green pepper — cored, seeds removed, and chopped
2 teaspoons oil
1/4 cup water or vegetable broth
1-1/2 cups rice, pre-cooked (leftovers are good)
3 large ripe tomatoes, cubed
8-ounce can tomato sauce
Pepper, cumin, and chili powder to taste

Sauté onion and green pepper in oil in a large frying pan over medium heat for 3 minutes. Add remaining ingredients and cook 10 more minutes, stirring occasionally to prevent sticking. Serve.

Total calories per serving: 222
Fat: 4 grams   Total Fat as % of Daily Value: 6%
Protein: 5 grams   Iron: 3 mg   Carbohydrate: 43 grams
Calcium: 29 mg   Dietary fiber: 4 grams

STUFFED MUSHROOMS
(Serves 4)

12 large mushrooms
1/2 cup vegetable broth or water
1 small ripe avocado
1 small ripe tomato, finely chopped
Pinch of cayenne pepper and garlic powder
Salt to taste

Remove stems from mushrooms. Sauté mushroom caps in broth or water for a few minutes until soft. Remove from heat and allow to cool. Mash avocado in a small bowl. Add tomato and seasonings. Mix well. Stuff mushrooms with avocado mixture and serve.

Total calories per serving: 90
Fat: 7 grams   Total Fat as % of Daily Value: 11%
Protein: 4 grams   Iron: 1 mg   Carbohydrate: 7 grams
Calcium: 8 mg   Dietary fiber: 1 gram

FRIED ZUCCHINI AND SAUCE
(Serves 4)

1 Tablespoon oil
2 pounds zucchini, sliced lengthwise ½-inch thick
Italian seasoning, salt, and pepper to taste
8-ounce can tomato sauce

Fry zucchini slices in oil in a large covered frying pan with seasonings for 5 minutes over medium heat. Flip zucchini over, cover with tomato sauce, and continue cooking over low heat for 10 minutes. Serve warm.

Total calories per serving: 78
Fat: 4 grams   Total Fat as % of Daily Value: 6%
Protein: 3 grams   Iron: 2 mg   Carbohydrate: 16 grams
Calcium: 41 mg   Dietary fiber: 3 grams

SWEET AND SOUR CABBAGE

(Serves 6)

1 small head cabbage (red and/or green), shredded
1 large onion, chopped
2 Tablespoons oil
1/2 cup raisins
1 large apple, grated
1/2 cup water
2 Tablespoons unbleached white flour
2 Tablespoons vinegar
1 Tablespoon brown sugar or other granulated sweetener
2 teaspoons salt
1/2 cup water

Sauté onions and cabbage in oil in a large frying pan over a medium heat for 8 minutes. Add raisins, apple, and 1/2 cup water. Cook 5 minutes longer. In a small jar, shake up flour, vinegar, sugar, salt, and 1/2 cup water. Add to frying pan and cook another 8 minutes. Serve warm.

Variation: Use crushed pineapple instead of grated apple.

Total calories per serving: 142
Fat: 5 grams   Total Fat as % of Daily Value: 8%
Protein: 2 grams   Iron: 1 mg   Carbohydrate: 25 grams
Calcium: 57 mg   Dietary fiber: 3 grams

PASTA DISH
(Serves 4)

3 Tablespoons vegan margarine
1/4 teaspoon each oregano, basil, salt, and black pepper
1/2 teaspoon garlic powder
1/4 cup fresh parsley, finely chopped (optional)
1 pound pasta, cooked and drained
3 Tablespoons vegan Parmesan cheese or nutritional yeast

Melt margarine in a large pot and add seasonings. Stir in cooked pasta, sprinkle on cheese or yeast and serve warm.

Total calories per serving: 509
Fat: 10 grams   Total Fat as % of Daily Value: 15%
Protein: 17 grams   Iron: 4 mg   Carbohydrate: 86 grams
Calcium: 69 mg   Dietary fiber: 0 grams

Main Dishes

RIGATONI COMBINATION
(Serves 6)

1/3 pound rigatoni shells, macaroni, or other pasta
1 large onion, chopped
1 clove garlic, minced
1/2 large green pepper, chopped
2 teaspoons olive oil
8-ounce can tomato sauce
16-ounce can kidney beans, drained
1 teaspoons soy sauce or tamari
1/2 teaspoon chili powder
Pepper and salt to taste

Cook pasta according to package directions. Sauté onion, garlic, and green pepper in oil for 5 minutes in a large pot. Stir in tomato sauce, kidney beans, soy sauce or tamari, and seasonings. Simmer several minutes to heat through. Drain pasta when done cooking and stir into sauce. Serve as is or add hot sauce if desired.

Total calories per serving: 181
Fat: 2 grams   Total Fat as % of Daily Value: 3%
Protein: 8 grams   Iron: 3 mg   Carbohydrate: 33 grams
Calcium: 36 mg   Dietary fiber: 6 grams

TOMATO/EGGPLANT BAKE
(Serves 4)

1 Tablespoon oil
1 small eggplant, peeled and cut into small pieces
15-ounce can stewed tomatoes
1 onion, finely chopped
1 large green pepper, finely chopped

Preheat oven to 350 degrees. Place eggplant, stewed tomatoes, onion, and green pepper in a large oiled baking dish. Bake at 350 degrees until done (approximately 20 minutes). Serve warm.

Total calories per serving: 100
Fat: 4 grams   Total Fat as % of Daily Value: 6%
Protein: 2 grams   Iron: 1 mg   Carbohydrate: 16 grams
Calcium: 54 mg   Dietary fiber: 3 grams

BROCCOLI/KASHA BAKE
(Serves 6)

10-ounce box frozen broccoli
1-1/2 cups kasha, uncooked
4 slices vegan cheese
1 Tablespoon oil

Preheat oven to 350 degrees. Cook broccoli per package directions and drain. Cook kasha in water until done. Mash broccoli and mix well with kasha. Place in a medium-size oiled baking dish. Lay slices of cheese on top. Bake at 350 degrees until cheese melts. Serve warm.

Total calories per serving: 205
Fat: 5 grams   Total Fat as % of Daily Value: 8%
Protein: 7 grams   Iron: 1 mg   Carbohydrate: 36 grams
Calcium: 156 mg   Dietary fiber: 5 grams

VEGETARIAN STEW
(Serves 4)

1/2 cup corn kernels (fresh, frozen, or canned)
1/2 cup lima beans (fresh, frozen, or canned)
1/2 cup potatoes (pre-cooked or canned)
1/2 cup stewed tomatoes
1 medium onion, chopped
1 teaspoon oregano
1/4 cup fresh parsley, finely chopped
Salt and pepper to taste

Mix above ingredients in a large pot. Cook over low heat until heated through (about 12 minutes). Serve alone or over rice.

Total calories per serving: 87
Fat: <1 gram   Total Fat as % of Daily Value: <1%
Protein: 3 grams   Iron: 1 mg   Carbohydrate: 15 grams
Calcium: 28 mg   Dietary fiber: 3 grams

LEFTOVER STEW
(Serves 4)

1 Tablespoon oil
1 small onion, chopped
1 green pepper, chopped
3 stalks celery, chopped
1 cup crushed tomatoes
2 cups leftovers (pre-cooked beans, seeds or nuts, raisins,
    grains, vegetables, olives, etc.)
Salt, pepper, and Italian seasoning to taste

Sauté onion, green pepper, and celery in oil in a large pot. Add tomatoes, leftovers, and seasonings. Cook over medium heat 10-15 minutes and serve warm.

Total calories per serving (using kidney beans and rice): 171
Fat: 4 grams   Total Fat as % of Daily Value: 6%
Protein: 6 grams   Iron: 2 mg   Carbohydrate: 29 grams
Calcium: 52 mg   Dietary fiber: 5 grams

MACARONI/CABBAGE DISH
(Serves 4)

1-1/2 cups macaroni
6 cups water
1/2 medium cabbage, shredded
1 medium onion, chopped
1 large green pepper, chopped
1/2 cup vegetable broth
Salt and pepper to taste

Cook macaroni in boiling water until tender and drain. Meanwhile, sauté cabbage, onion, and green pepper in vegetable broth in a large pot over medium heat for 10 minutes. Add cooked macaroni and seasoning and heat 5 minutes longer. Serve warm.

Total calories per serving: 187
Fat: 1 gram   Total Fat as % of Daily Value: 2%
Protein: 7 grams   Iron: 2 mg   Carbohydrate: 39 grams
Calcium: 59 mg   Dietary fiber: 3 grams

VEGETABLE POT PIE
(Serves 8)

Crust: This is a quick crust that can be used in many different recipes. (In a rush use a store-bought pie crust.)

2 cups whole wheat pastry flour or unbleached white flour
1/2 teaspoon salt
1/2 cup vegan margarine
1/2 cup water

Mix flour and salt in bowl. Work in margarine with fingers. Add water, stirring as little as possible to form a ball. Divide into 2 equal balls and roll out to 1/8-inch thickness. Prick pie shells and bake in pie pans at 400 degrees for 10 minutes.

Vegetable Filling:

1/2 cup vegetable broth
1 cup onions, chopped
1 cup celery, chopped
1/2 cup carrots, chopped
1-1/4 cups peas (fresh or frozen)

Sauté above ingredients in broth until onions are soft. In a separate bowl mix the following:

1/4 cup oil
1/2 cup unbleached white flour
1-2/3 cups water
1/2 teaspoon garlic powder
1 teaspoon salt
1/3 teaspoon pepper

Preheat oven to 350 degrees. Add above mixture to sautéed vegetables. Pour into one pie shell and cover with the other pie shell. Bake at 350 degrees until crust is brown (approximately 15-20 minutes).

Total calories per serving: 320
Fat: 18 grams   Total Fat as % of Daily Value: 28%
Protein: 7 grams   Iron: 2 mg   Carbohydrate: 34 grams
Calcium: 33 mg   Dietary fiber: 6 grams

VEGETARIAN CHILI
(Serves 6)

1 Tablespoon oil
1 large onion, chopped
3 cloves garlic, minced
1 large green pepper, chopped
3 cups water
1 cup kidney beans (pre-cooked or canned)
4 large ripe tomatoes, chopped
1 cup corn kernels (fresh, frozen, or canned)
1 teaspoon salt
1 teaspoon chili powder
Pepper to taste

In a large pot sauté the onion, garlic, and green pepper in oil over medium heat until the onion is soft. Add water, kidney beans, tomatoes, corn, salt, chili powder, and pepper. Cook 25 minutes longer.

Variations: Add hot peppers, other vegetables such as carrots and celery, or add 2/3 cup bulgur (cracked wheat). Pinto beans may be used instead of kidney beans.

Total calories per serving: 118
Fat: 3 grams   Total Fat as % of Daily Value: 5%
Protein: 5 grams   Iron: 1 mg   Carbohydrate: 15 grams
Calcium: 28 mg   Dietary fiber: 5 grams

RATATOUILLE
(Serves 4)

1/2 cup vegetable broth
3 large ripe tomatoes, chopped
1 large zucchini, chopped
1 small eggplant, cubed
1 large green pepper, chopped
1 large onion, chopped
2-3 cloves garlic, minced

In a large frying pan sauté the tomatoes, zucchini, eggplant, peppers, onions, and garlic in broth over low heat for 15 minutes. Serve warm over a bed of rice or slice of bread.

Total calories per serving: 81
Fat: 1 gram   Total Fat as % of Daily Value: 2%
Protein: 3 grams   Iron: 1 mg   Carbohydrate: 18 grams
Calcium: 36 mg   Dietary fiber: 3 grams

SPAGHETTI AND VEGETABLE SAUCE
(Serves 4)

Cook 1 pound of spaghetti and drain.

Sauce:

2 teaspoons oil
1 large onion, chopped
2 cloves garlic, minced
15-ounce can tomato sauce
6-ounce can tomato paste
1 small zucchini, sliced
2 carrots, chopped
1 cup mushrooms, sliced
Italian seasoning, salt, and pepper to taste

Sauté onion and garlic in oil in a large pot over low heat for 5 minutes. Add sauce, paste, vegetables, and seasoning. Cook 20 minutes longer. Serve warm over cooked pasta.

Total calories per serving: 529
Fat: 5 grams   Total Fat as % of Daily Value: 8%
Protein: 18 grams   Iron: 8 mg   Carbohydrate: 104 grams
Calcium: 65 mg   Dietary fiber: 7 grams

FRIED EGGPLANT
(Serves 4)

1 large eggplant
1/4 cup oil
1 cup bread crumbs (or crushed corn flakes or matzo meal)
1 medium onion, chopped
3 cloves garlic, minced

Slice eggplant. Add one Tablespoon oil to bread crumbs. Dip eggplant slices into crumbs. Fry eggplant, onion, and garlic in remaining oil over medium heat for 10 minutes.

Variations: Top with vegan parmesan cheese, tomato sauce, and/or Italian seasoning.

Total calories per serving: 269
Fat: 15 grams   Total Fat as % of Daily Value: 23%
Protein: 5 grams   Iron: 1 mg   Carbohydrate: 30 grams
Calcium: 50 mg   Dietary fiber: 1 gram

LENTIL STEW
(Serves 6)

1 cup lentils
1 cup macaroni or other pasta
15-ounce can tomato sauce
6-ounce can tomato paste
1 large onion, chopped
1 teaspoon Italian seasoning
1 teaspoon garlic powder
4 cups water

Cook all ingredients in a large pot over medium heat until tender
(approximately 20 minutes). Serve warm.

Total calories per serving: 203
Fat: 1 gram   Total Fat as % of Daily Value: 2%
Protein: 11 grams   Iron: 5 mg   Carbohydrate: 39 grams
Calcium: 40 mg   Dietary fiber: 7 grams

ZUCCHINI BAKE
(Serves 4)

2 large zucchini, sliced
4 slices vegan cheese
15-ounce can tomato sauce
Salt and pepper to taste

Preheat oven to 325 degrees. Place alternating layers of zucchini,
cheese, and tomato sauce in a medium-size baking dish. Season
to taste. Bake at 325 degrees for 20-25 minutes. Serve hot.

Total calories per serving: 95
Fat: 3 grams   Total Fat as % of Daily Value: 5%
Protein: 4 grams   Iron: 2 mg   Carbohydrate: 14 grams
Calcium: 222 mg   Dietary fiber:3 grams

Soy Dishes

Although tofu and tempeh may not be familiar products to you, we have chosen to include them because they are convenient soy food products. Tofu can be found in most supermarkets today. If you've eaten in Chinese restaurants, you probably have eaten some tofu. It would have been called soybean curd. Tofu can be used to make dips and soups, desserts such as strawberry tofu cheesecake, and side or main dishes such as curried tofu or fried tofu, which has a texture similar to fried chicken. Unfortunately, tempeh is still only found in some supermarkets and is more likely to be found in a natural foods store. It is a fermented soy product and has a meaty texture. Tempeh can be prepared in a variety of ways.

TOFU MAYONNAISE DIP
(Serves 8)

16-ounces tofu, drained (soft or silken tofu is best)
1/2 teaspoon prepared mustard
2 teaspoons lemon juice
1 Tablespoon olive or vegetable oil
3 Tablespoons water
1 large clove garlic, minced
1/4 teaspoon salt
1 Tablespoon soy sauce or tamari
1/2 teaspoon Louisiana-style hot sauce (optional)
1/2 teaspoon rice or maple syrup (optional)

Blend all the ingredients in a food processor until very smooth. Use as a dressing for potato, macaroni, or rice salads; or use as a dip for raw vegetables. If you want a simple mayonnaise, omit the last four ingredients.

Total calories per serving: 48
Fat: 3 grams   Total Fat as % of Daily Value: 5%
Protein: 3 grams   Iron: 1 mg   Carbohydrate: 2 grams
Calcium: 17 mg   Dietary fiber: <1 gram

TOFU SPINACH DIP
(Serves 8)

1 large onion, finely chopped
2 cloves garlic, minced
2 Tablespoons oil
1/2 pound tofu, drained (soft or silken tofu is best)
3 Tablespoons mustard or eggless mayonnaise
10-ounce box frozen spinach, pre-cooked
Dash of pepper
Soy sauce or tamari to taste

Sauté onion and garlic in oil in a large frying pan over medium heat for 5 minutes. Pour into a blender cup and add remaining ingredients. Blend until creamy. Chill and serve with crackers and/or raw vegetables.

Total calories per serving: 67
Fat: 5 grams   Total Fat as % of Daily Value: 8%
Protein: 3 grams   Iron: 1 mg   Carbohydrate: 5 grams
Calcium: 69 mg   Dietary fiber: 1 gram

TOFU EGGLESS SALAD
(Serves 6)

1 pound tofu, drained and crumbled (firm tofu is best)
1 stalk celery, finely chopped
1 large carrot, grated
3 Tablespoons sweet pickle relish
2 Tablespoons eggless mayonnaise
Salt, pepper, and dill weed to taste

In a medium-size bowl mix all the ingredients together. Serve on a bed of lettuce or on whole grain toast with lettuce and sprouts.

Total calories per serving: 117
Fat: 6 grams   Total Fat as % of Daily Value: 9%
Protein: 9 grams   Iron: 1 mg   Carbohydrate: 6 grams
Calcium: 139 mg   Dietary fiber: 1 gram

SUMMER TOFU SALAD
(Serves 4)

1/2 pound romaine lettuce leaves, rinsed
1 pound tofu, drained and cut in finger-size pieces (soft or silken tofu is best)
1 stalk celery, chopped
2 scallions, chopped
1 large white radish, chopped
1/4 cup fresh parsley, finely chopped
1 large ripe tomato, chopped
1 Tablespoon soy sauce or tamari
1 teaspoon oil
Salt and pepper to taste

Lay lettuce leaves on 4 small plates. Arrange pieces of tofu around perimeter of each plate leaving an empty circle in the middle. Sprinkle with celery, scallions, radish, and parsley. Put tomato in center of each plate. Drizzle soy sauce or tamari and oil over the entire dish. Season and serve.

Hint: This salad tastes better if it sits a while before serving.

Total calories per serving: 98
Fat: 5 grams   Total Fat as % of Daily Value: 8%
Protein: 7 grams   Iron: 2 mg   Carbohydrate: 8 grams
Calcium: 69 mg   Dietary fiber: 2 grams

SPINACH PIE
(Serves 8)

10-ounce box frozen spinach
1-1/2 cups onion, chopped
3 cloves garlic, minced
2 Tablespoons oil
3 cups crumbled tofu (soft or silken tofu is best)
1 Tablespoon lemon juice
Salt and pepper to taste
1 pre-made pie crust

Cook spinach according to package directions. Sauté onion and garlic in oil in a large pot over medium heat for 3 minutes. Add spinach, tofu, lemon juice, and seasoning. Preheat oven to 350 degrees. Meanwhile, continue cooking spinach/tofu mixture for 5 minutes. Mix well. Pour into pie crust. Bake at 350 degrees for 15-20 minutes until crust is brown.

Total calories per serving: 180
Fat: 11 grams   Total Fat as % of Daily Value: 18%
Protein: 7 grams   Iron: 2 mg   Carbohydrate: 15 grams
Calcium: 87 mg   Dietary fiber: 1 gram

TOFU BURGERS
(Serves 4)

2 cups tofu, crumbled (firm tofu is best)
2 teaspoons garlic powder
1 cup wheat germ
2 teaspoons onion powder
2 Tablespoons soy sauce or tamari
1 teaspoon pepper
1/2 cup fresh parsley, finely chopped
1/2 cup celery, finely chopped
1 Tablespoon oil
1/2 cup water or vegetable broth
2 teaspoons oil for frying

Blend or mash tofu well and add remaining ingredients (except 2 teaspoons oil for frying). (The easiest way to do this is in a food processor, but you can do it by hand.) Mix well. Form patties and fry in a lightly oiled frying pan on both sides until brown (approximately 10 minutes). Serve warm on whole grain bread with lettuce and sliced tomato. Cold leftover burgers are also good.

Variation: Bake burgers instead of frying by first rolling patties in wheat germ. Lay in baking pan and bake at 350 degrees until warm and light brown.

Total calories per serving: 318
Fat: 16 grams   Total Fat as % of Daily Value: 25%
Protein: 24 grams   Iron: 5 mg   Carbohydrate: 19 grams
Calcium: 256 mg   Dietary fiber: <1 gram

FRIED TOFU
(Serves 4)

1 pound tofu, drained and sliced
1/4 cup soy sauce or tamari
1 cup unbleached white flour
2 Tablespoons oil
Salt and pepper to taste

Dip tofu in soy sauce or tamari, then in flour. Season well with salt and pepper, then fry in oil over medium heat in a large frying pan until brown on both sides (approximately 10-15 minutes). Serve warm as is or as a sandwich on whole grain bread with lettuce and tomato.

Variations: Instead of unbleached white flour, use wheat germ or nutritional yeast.

Total calories per serving: 271
Fat: 13 grams   Total Fat as % of Daily Value: 20%
Protein: 14 grams   Iron: 8 mg   Carbohydrate: 27 grams
Calcium: 127 mg   Dietary fiber: 1 gram

CURRIED TOFU WITH PEANUTS
(Serves 4)

1 large onion, finely chopped
2 cloves garlic, minced
3 Tablespoons oil
1/4 cup roasted peanuts, whole or chopped
1 pound tofu, drained and cut into 1-inch cubes
1 teaspoon salt
1 teaspoon curry powder
1-1/2 cups peas (fresh, frozen, or canned)
1 large carrot, chopped

Sauté onion and garlic in oil in large frying pan over medium heat for 3 minutes. Add remaining ingredients and cook for 15 minutes longer. Add a little water if necessary to prevent sticking. Serve warm over a bed of rice.

Variations: Use garlic powder or minced ginger instead of garlic. Also, use different nuts and vegetables.

Total calories per serving: 299
Fat: 20 grams   Total Fat as % of Daily Value: 30%
Protein: 15 grams   Iron: 7 mg   Carbohydrate: 18 grams
Calcium: 156 mg   Dietary fiber: 4 grams

FRIED TEMPEH SANDWICHES
(Serves 4)

8-ounce package tempeh (any variety), sliced into strips
2 Tablespoons oil
1 medium onion, chopped
Salt and pepper to taste
8 slices whole grain bread

Fry tempeh in oil with onions and seasoning over medium heat in a large frying pan until brown on both sides (approximately 10 minutes). Place tempeh and onions on whole grain bread with sliced tomato, cucumber, mayonnaise or mustard, sprouts, and lettuce.

Total calories per serving (not including tomato, etc.): 322
Fat: 14 grams   Total Fat as % of Daily Value: 22%
Protein: 16 grams   Iron: 3 mg   Carbohydrate: 38 grams
Calcium: 98 mg   Dietary fiber: <1 gram

SPAGHETTI AND TEMPEH SAUCE
(Serves 4)

1 pound spaghetti, pre-cooked and drained

Sauce:

**8-ounce package tempeh (any variety), chopped into 1-inch
   cubes**
1/2 teaspoon oregano
Garlic powder and salt to taste
1 small onion, finely chopped (optional)
2 Tablespoons oil
8-ounce can tomato sauce

Sauté tempeh in oil with seasoning and chopped onion if desired in a large frying pan over medium heat for 5 minutes. Add tomato sauce and heat 5 minutes longer. Serve warm over cooked spaghetti.

Total calories per serving: 408
Fat: 13 grams   Total Fat as % of Daily Value: 20%
Protein: 26 grams   Iron: 6 mg   Carbohydrate: 98 grams
Calcium: 80 mg   Dietary fiber: 1 gram

Chinese Cuisine

CHINESE MIXED VEGETABLES AND TOFU
(Serves 5)

2 Tablespoons oil
1/2 cup vegetable broth
2 cups vegetables, chopped (i.e. celery, carrots, green
    pepper, bok choy, corn, snow peas)
8 ounces tofu, drained and cubed (firm tofu is best)
Soy sauce or tamari to taste

Stir-fry ingredients in oil and broth in a large frying pan over medium heat for 15 minutes. Serve alone or over a bed of rice.

Total calories per serving (celery, carrots, green pepper, and bok choy): 115
Fat: 8 grams   Total Fat as % of Daily Value: 12%
Protein: 6 grams   Iron: 1 mg   Carbohydrate: 5 grams
Calcium: 93 mg   Dietary fiber: 1 gram

STIR-FRIED VEGETABLES, GINGER, AND RICE
(Serves 6)

1 Tablespoon oil
1/3 cup vegetable broth
3 cups mixed vegetables, chopped
1-1/2 cups pre-cooked rice (leftovers are good)
2 Tablespoons soy sauce or tamari
1/4 teaspoon fresh ginger, grated

Sauté vegetables in oil and broth in a large pot over medium heat for 10 minutes. Add rice, soy sauce or tamari, and ginger to vegetables. Cook 8 minutes longer and serve warm.

Total calories per serving (using broccoli, carrots, and cabbage): 96
Fat: 3 grams   Total Fat as % of Daily Value: 5%
Protein: 3 grams   Iron: 1 mg   Carbohydrate: 16 grams
Calcium: 25 mg   Dietary fiber: 2 grams

VEGETABLE CHOW MEIN
(Serves 6)

2 Tablespoons oil
1/2 cup vegetable broth
3 cups pre-cooked rice (leftovers are good)
1 cup bean sprouts (fresh or canned)
1 stalk celery, chopped
1 large green pepper, chopped
1 large carrot, chopped
2 large ripe tomatoes, chopped
Soy sauce or tamari to taste

Sauté the rice and vegetables with soy sauce or tamari in oil and broth in a large frying pan over medium heat for 15 minutes. Serve warm.

Total calories per serving: 176
Fat: 6 grams   Total Fat as % of Daily Value: 9%
Protein: 3 grams   Iron: 1 mg   Carbohydrate: 29 grams
Calcium: 23 mg   Dietary fiber: 3 grams

MOCK FOO YOUNG
(Serves 2)

10 ounces tofu, crumbled (firm tofu is best)
1/4 cup cornmeal
1 large carrot, grated
Salt and pepper to taste
1/4 teaspoon oregano
1 Tablespoon sesame seeds (optional)
2 teaspoons oil for frying

Blend all the ingredients (except oil for frying) together in a blender. Form four patties and fry on both sides until light brown in a lightly oiled frying pan over medium heat.

Variation: For a totally different taste, cover patties with tomato sauce and sprinkle with vegan cheese.

Total calories per serving: 288
Fat: 13 grams   Total Fat as % of Daily Value: 20%
Protein: 18 grams   Iron: 3 mg   Carbohydrate: 16 grams
Calcium: 260 mg   Dietary fiber: 2 grams

FRIED RICE WITH PEANUTS OR ALMONDS
(Serves 6)

1 large onion, chopped
1 Tablespoon oil
2 cups pre-cooked rice (leftovers are good)
1 large green pepper, chopped
1 stalk celery, chopped
1 cup mushrooms, sliced
1 small zucchini, chopped
2 Tablespoons soy sauce or tamari
1 cup roasted peanuts or almonds, chopped or whole

Sauté onion in oil in a large frying pan over a medium heat for 3 minutes. Add the remaining ingredients and stir-fry 15 minutes.

Total calories per serving: 256
Fat: 15 grams   Total Fat as % of Daily Value: 23%
Protein: 9 grams   Iron: 1 mg   Carbohydrate: 25 grams
Calcium: 42 mg   Dietary fiber: 4 grams

Mexican Fiesta

MEXICAN SUCCOTASH
(Serves 6)

2 Tablespoons oil
1 small onion, chopped
1 pound zucchini, sliced
1 large green pepper, chopped
1/4 cup pimientos, diced
2 large ripe tomatoes, chopped
1-1/2 cups corn kernels (frozen, fresh, or canned)
Salt and pepper to taste

Sauté onion in oil in a large frying pan over medium heat for 3 minutes. Add remaining ingredients and simmer until vegetables are tender (about 10 minutes). Add a little water if necessary to prevent sticking. Serve as a side dish or over a bed of rice.

Total calories per serving: 112
Fat: 5 grams   Total Fat as % of Daily Value: 8%
Protein: 3 grams   Iron: 1 mg   Carbohydrate: 8 grams
Calcium: 18 mg   Dietary fiber: 3 grams

REFRIED BEANS
(Serves 8)

1 large onion, chopped
3 Tablespoons oil
Two 15-ounce cans pinto or kidney beans, drained
6-ounce can tomato paste
3 Tablespoons chili powder

Sauté onion in oil in a large frying pan over a medium heat for three minutes. Add the remaining ingredients and stir-fry for 15 minutes. Serve over tortilla chips or in taco shells with shredded lettuce, chopped tomatoes, hot sauce, olives, etc.

Total calories per serving: 162
Fat: 6 grams   Total Fat as % of Daily Value: 9%
Protein: 6 grams   Iron: 3 mg   Carbohydrate: 22 grams
Calcium: 57 mg   Dietary fiber: 2 grams

EASY TOSTADAS
(Serves 6-8)

Two 1-pound cans vegetarian chili
1 box vegan enchilada shells or flat taco shells
1 cup shredded lettuce
1 large cucumber, peeled and chopped
1 large onion, chopped
1/2 cup shredded vegan cheese (optional)
Taco sauce to taste

Heat chili in a large pot until warm. Preheat oven to 400 degrees. Lay shells in a single layer on a cookie sheet. Spread chili on each shell. Heat at 400 degrees for 5 minutes. Remove from oven and let each person garnish shells with remaining ingredients as desired. Note: This dish tastes good chilled as well. Simply open can and put chili on shells and garnish. This is a terrific dish when traveling.

Total calories per serving: 278
Fat: 2 grams   Total Fat as % of Daily Value: 3%
Protein: 15 grams   Iron: 4 mg   Carbohydrate: 51 grams
Calcium: 103 mg   Dietary fiber: 13 grams

GUACAMOLE
(Serves 4)

1 large or 2 small ripe avocados, peeled and pit(s) removed
1 small ripe tomato, finely chopped
1/4 teaspoon garlic powder
Pinch of cayenne pepper
Salt to taste

Mash avocado in a bowl. Add chopped tomato and seasonings. Mix well and serve on tacos, with chips or crackers, or as a dip with raw vegetables.

Total calories per serving: 100
Fat: 9 grams   Total Fat as % of Daily Value: 14%
Protein: 1 gram   Iron: 1 mg   Carbohydrate: 5 grams
Calcium: 7 mg   Dietary fiber: 2 grams

Spreads and Dips

Spreads can be used for parties, snacks, or light dinners. They not only taste good, but can be nutritious. But like many foods, if you eat too much, the calories will add up. Serve these spreads and dips with lowfat crackers, breads, or raw vegetables such as carrots, celery, peppers, cauliflower, or zucchini.

LENTIL PATE
(Serves 8)

1 cup lentils
2 cups water
1 large onion, finely chopped
4 cloves garlic, minced
1 Tablespoon vegan margarine
1 teaspoon black pepper
1/2 teaspoon vinegar
Water if necessary

Cook lentils in water in a medium-size pot until done. At the same time, sauté onions and garlic in margarine in a separate pot over medium heat for 3 minutes. Add pepper. Mix lentils, onions, garlic, and pepper together. Blend the mixture in a food processor adding water if necessary until well mixed. Add vinegar last. Chill before serving.

Total calories per serving: 85
Fat: 2 grams   Total Fat as % of Daily Value: 3%
Protein: 5 grams   Iron: 2 mg   Carbohydrate: 13 grams
Calcium: 17 mg   Dietary fiber: 3 grams

MUSHROOM/EGGPLANT SPREAD
(Makes about 4 cups)

1 pound eggplant, peeled and chopped into 1-inch cubes
12 ounces portabello mushrooms, finely chopped
Medium onion, finely chopped
2 Tablespoons oil
1/2 teaspoon coriander
1/2 teaspoon cumin
Salt and pepper to taste

Sauté ingredients in a large frying pan over medium-high heat for 10-12 minutes. Mash with a potato masher until a chunky, yet spreadable consistency. Chill and spread on crackers or bread.

Total calories per ¼ cup serving: 30
Fat: 2 grams   Total Fat as % of Daily Value: 3%
Protein: 1 gram   Iron: <1 mg   Carbohydrate: 3 grams
Calcium: 4 mg   Dietary fiber: <1 gram

GARBANZO PEANUT SPREAD
(Serves 8)

16-ounce can chickpeas, drained
3 Tablespoons peanut butter
1/3 cup lemon juice
3/4 cup water or as needed
1 Tablespoon oil
1/8 teaspoon cumin
1/2 teaspoon garlic powder
Salt and pepper to taste

Blend all the ingredients together in a food processor until smooth. Add more water if necessary.

Variation: Instead of using peanut butter, use tahini (sesame butter) and add some sautéed onions and parsley.

Total calories per serving: 125
Fat: 6 grams   Total Fat as % of Daily Value: 9%
Protein: 5 grams   Iron: 1 mg   Carbohydrate: 14 grams
Calcium: 27 mg   Dietary fiber: 5 grams

SPLIT PEA SPREAD
(Serves 6)

1 cup split peas
3-1/4 cups water
1 large carrot, finely chopped
2 stalks celery, finely chopped
1 small onion, finely chopped
1 teaspoon celery seed
Salt and pepper to taste

Bring split peas to a rapid boil in a medium-size pot. Add carrot and celery. Then add onions and seasoning. Cover pot and boil 15 minutes longer. Remove from heat and blend until smooth in a food processor.   Place in a bowl and chill before serving.

Total calories per serving: 125
Fat: <1 gram   Total Fat as % of Daily Value: <1%
Protein: 8 grams   Iron: 2 mg   Carbohydrate: 23 grams
Calcium: 30 mg   Dietary fiber: 2 grams

CHOPPED "LIVER" SPREAD
(Serves 6)

1 Tablespoon oil
1/4 cup water
1/2 pound mushrooms, chopped
1 small onion, chopped
1 cup chopped walnuts
Salt and pepper to taste

Sauté mushrooms and onion in oil and water in a large frying pan over medium heat for 8 minutes. Pour into a food processor. Add walnuts and seasoning. Blend until smooth, adding more water if necessary. Chill before serving.

Total calories per serving: 115
Fat: 10 grams   Total Fat as % of Daily Value: 17%
Protein: 4 grams   Iron: 1 mg   Carbohydrate: 4 grams
Calcium: 12 mg   Dietary fiber: 1 gram

WHITE BEAN SPREAD
(Makes about 2 cups)

19-ounce can white beans, drained
1 stalk celery, finely chopped
Juice of 1/2 small lemon
1/4 teaspoon dill weed
Pepper to taste

Mash white beans in a bowl. Add remaining ingredients and mix well. Chill before serving.

Total calories per ¼ cup serving: 78
Fat: <1 gram   Total Fat as % of Daily Value: <1%
Protein: 5 grams   Iron: 1 mg   Carbohydrate: 14 grams
Calcium: 34 mg   Dietary fiber: 3 grams

AVOCADO/CUCUMBER SPREAD
(Serves 8)

1 small ripe avocado, pit removed
1 large cucumber, peeled and chopped
1/4 teaspoon garlic powder
1/4 teaspoon salt
1/4 teaspoon cayenne

Place all the ingredients in a food processor and blend until creamy. This spread can also be used as a salad dressing.

Total calories per serving: 35
Fat: 3 grams   Total Fat as % of Daily Value: 5%
Protein: 1 gram   Iron: <1 mg   Carbohydrate: 2 grams
Calcium: 8 mg   Dietary fiber: 1 gram

NUT "CHEESE"
(Serves 6)

1/2 cup raw cashews
1/2 cup water
1/4 cup lemon juice
3 Tablespoons oil
1/2 small tomato, finely chopped
Garlic powder and paprika to taste

Blend cashews, water, and lemon juice together in a food processor. Slowly add oil. Then add remaining ingredients and blend well. Chill before serving.

Total calories per serving: 130
Fat: 12 grams   Total Fat as % of Daily Value: 18%
Protein: 2 grams   Iron: 1 mg   Carbohydrate: 5 grams
Calcium: 7 mg   Dietary fiber: 1 gram

Desserts

SPICY DATE NUT SPREAD
(Serves 4)

1/4 pound dates, pitted
1/2 cup hot water
1/2 cup walnuts, chopped
1 large apple, cored and finely chopped
1/4 teaspoon cinnamon
Pinch of ginger powder (optional)

Soak dates in hot water for a few minutes. Put date/water mixture in a food processor. Add remaining ingredients and blend until smooth. Serve on slices of fresh fruit including apples, peaches, and pears.

Total calories per serving: 169
Fat: 6 grams   Total Fat as % of Daily Value: 9%
Protein: 3 grams   Iron: 1 mg   Carbohydrate: 30 grams
Calcium: 19 mg   Dietary fiber: 4 grams

COCONUT CLUSTERS
(Serves 8)

2 cups shredded coconut
4 ripe medium bananas, mashed
1/4 cup cocoa powder or carob powder
1 cup walnuts, chopped (optional)

Preheat oven to 350 degrees. Blend ingredients together in a medium-size bowl. Form clusters on a lightly oiled cookie sheet. Bake for 20 minutes at 350 degrees. Cool, then remove from cookie sheet.

Variation: Instead of cocoa or carob powder, use 1/2 cup chopped fresh fruit such as strawberries.

Total calories per serving: 174
Fat: 9 grams   Total Fat as % of Daily Value: 14%
Protein: 2 grams   Iron: 2 mg   Carbohydrate: 26 grams
Calcium: 11 mg   Dietary fiber: 2 grams

OATMEAL COOKIES
(Makes 40 cookies)

1/2 cup vegan margarine
1-1/2 cups (15 ounces) applesauce
1/2 cup molasses or maple syrup
2 large ripe bananas, peeled
1-3/4 cups whole wheat pastry flour
1 teaspoon baking soda
1 teaspoon baking powder
1 teaspoon cinnamon
1 teaspoon nutmeg
3 cups rolled oats
1/2 cup raisins or chopped dates

Preheat oven to 400 degrees. Cream together margarine, applesauce, molasses or maple syrup, and bananas in a large bowl. Add remaining ingredients and mix well. Drop a rounded Tablespoon of batter at a time on a lightly oiled cookie sheet. Bake 8 minutes at 400 degrees. Allow cookies to cool before removing from cookie sheet.

Variation: Add chopped walnuts or chopped apples to batter.

Total calories per cookie: 84
Fat: 3 grams   Total Fat as % of Daily Value: 5%
Protein: 2 grams   Iron: 1 mg   Carbohydrate: 15 grams
Calcium: 24 mg   Dietary fiber: 1 gram

FRESH FRUIT SALAD AND PEANUT CREME
(Serves 8)

Prepare a fruit salad for 8 people using your favorite fruits in season. If you are in a rush, use canned fruit salad.

Peanut Creme:

1 cup water
2 apples
1 cup peanuts

Blend apples in 1/2 cup water in a food processor. Slowly add peanuts and remaining water as needed until a smooth consistency is reached. Serve over fruit salad.

Total calories per serving (without fruit): 125
Fat: 9 grams   Total Fat as % of Daily Value: 14%
Protein: 5 grams   Iron: <1 mg   Carbohydrate: 9 grams
Calcium: 18 mg   Dietary fiber: 2 grams

Variations: Serve peanut creme over baked apples and pears. You can also experiment with different types of nuts.

RICE PUDDING
(Serves 6)

1 cup rice
2/3 cups raisins
2 large ripe bananas, peeled and mashed
1/2 cup water
1 teaspoon cinnamon
1/4 teaspoon nutmeg

Cook rice with raisins following package instructions in a large pot until done. Preheat oven to 350 degrees. Pour cooked rice and raisins into a food processor. Add the remaining ingredients and blend together for 1 minute. Pour into a medium-size baking dish. Bake for 20 minutes at 350 degrees. Serve warm or chilled.

Total calories per serving: 209
Fat: <1 gram   Total Fat as % of Daily Value: <1%
Protein: 3 grams   Iron: 2 mg   Carbohydrate: 50 grams
Calcium: 14 mg   Dietary fiber: 2 grams

TOFU PIE AND QUICK CRUST
(Serves 8)

Pie crust:

2 cups lowfat granola
1/4 cup vegan margarine

Preheat oven to 350 degrees. Blend granola and margarine together in a medium-size bowl. Press into 8-inch pie pan and bake for 10 minutes at 350 degrees. Leave oven on while you prepare pie filling below.

Pie filling:

4 dates
1 pound tofu, drained (soft or silken tofu is best)
3 Tablespoons chocolate syrup
2 Tablespoons oil

Soak dates in a little boiling water for 5 minutes and drain. Place pie filling ingredients in a blender cup and blend until creamy, adding a little water if necessary.

Pour filling into pie crust and bake for 20 minutes at 350 degrees. Chill in the refrigerator before serving.

Variation: Instead of chocolate syrup use fresh chopped fruit such as strawberries, peaches, or blueberries.

Total calories per serving: 231
Fat: 12 grams   Total Fat as % of Daily Value: 18%
Protein: 6 grams   Iron: 2 mg   Carbohydrate: 28 grams
Calcium: 30 mg   Dietary fiber: 2 grams

Seasonal Party Ideas for Twelve People

SUMMERTIME MENU:

Fruit Salad (recipe below)

2 dozen bagels and/or rolls with vegan cream cheese (such as *Tofutti* brand) or vegan margarine

Raw vegetable Platter (recipe below)

Guacamole (see page 151) or Avacado/Cucumber Spread (see page 156)

2 pounds assortment of nuts and seeds

2 pounds variety of dried fruit

2 gallons fruit juices and/or Blended Fruit Drink (see page 104)

1-1/2 dozen ears hot steamed corn (can be done indoors or out-doors over a barbecue)

FRUIT SALAD
(Serves 12)

1/2 ripe watermelon, cut lengthwise
10 peaches, pits removed and quartered
1 pint strawberries, sliced
1 pint blueberries
1 cup raisins
1 cup shredded coconut (optional)

Scoop out bite-size pieces of watermelon and place in a large bowl. Add remaining ingredients. Mix well and pour back into hollowed out watermelon shell. Keep chilled until serving.

Total calories per serving: 126
Fat: 1 gram   Total Fat as % of Daily Value: 2%
Protein: 2 grams   Iron: 1 mg   Carbohydrate: 31 grams
Calcium: 24 mg   Dietary fiber: 4 grams

RAW VEGETABLE PLATTER
(Serves 12)

5 large ripe tomatoes, sliced
1 pound carrots, sliced lengthwise into sticks
3 cucumbers, peeled and sliced
4 stalks celery, sliced lengthwise into sticks
1 pound olives, drained
1 pound chopped broccoli or cauliflower
1 pound zucchini, sliced lengthwise into sticks

Arrange all the vegetables on a large platter.

Total calories per serving: 120
Fat: 9 grams   Total Fat as % of Daily Value: 14%
Protein: 4 grams   Iron: 2 mg   Carbohydrate: 14 grams
Calcium: 91 mg   Dietary fiber: 5 grams

AUTUMN MENU:

Creamed Carrot Soup (see page 116 and double the recipe)
Ratatouille (see page 136 and double the recipe)
4 cups rice precooked
Curried Tofu with Peanuts (see page 144 and triple the recipe)
1 dozen fresh apples (assorted colors if possible)
2 gallons apple cider or apple juice
Oatmeal cookies (see page 158 and double the recipe)

WINTER MENU:

Vegetarian Chili (see page 135 and triple the recipe)
24 taco shells
2 large bags corn chips
Small head lettuce, shredded
1 pound vegan cheese, shredded
2 large onions, finely chopped
Large bottle hot sauce
12 large baked potatoes
Hot Apple Cider (see page 104 and double the recipe)
Coconut Clusters (see page 157 and double the recipe)

SPRING MENU:

Tofu Eggless Salad (see page 140 and double the recipe)
Mock "Tuna" Salad (see page 118 and double the recipe)
Cucumber Salad (see page 108 and double the recipe)
2 large boxes vegan bread sticks
White Bean Spread (see page 155 and double the recipe)
2 large loaves whole wheat bread and 1-1/2 dozen rolls
6 tangerines
6 oranges
6 large bananas
2 pints strawberries
6 apples
2 gallons assorted fruit juices

Vegan Meal Plan

If you are in doubt about your diet, you can use this plan prepared by Ruth Ransom, R.D. and updated by Reed Mangels, Ph.D, R.D. as a <u>GENERAL GUIDE</u>. Consult a dietitian or medical doctor knowledgeable about nutrition for special needs.

A. PROTEIN FOODS: 5-6 SERVINGS PER DAY (7 FOR PREGNANT WOMEN; 8 FOR BREASTFEEDING WOMEN)

1. one serving equals:
   - 1/2 cup cooked dried beans or peas
   - 1/2 cup cooked soybeans*
   - 1/2 cup tofu
   - 1/2 cup tofu with calcium* (read label)
   - 1/2 cup tempeh*
   - 1 cup calcium-fortified soymilk** (counts as 2 starred food items)
   - 1/4 cup almonds*, cashews, walnuts, pecans, or peanuts
   - 2 Tablespoons peanut butter, tahini*, or almond butter*
   - 1 ounce meat analog (veggie burger, veggie dog, deli slices, etc.)
   - 1/4 cup soynuts*

B. WHOLE GRAINS: AT LEAST 6-8 SERVINGS/DAY

1. one serving equals:
   - 1 slice whole wheat, rye, or whole grain bread
   - 1 buckwheat or whole wheat pancakes or waffle
   - 1 two-inch piece cornbread
   - 2 Tablespoons wheat germ
   - 1 ounce wheat or oat bran
   - 1/4 cup sunflower*, sesame, or pumpkin seeds
   - 3/4 cup wheat, bran, or corn flakes
   - 1/2 cup oatmeal or farina
   - 1/2 cup cooked brown rice, barley, bulgur, or corn
   - 1/2 cup whole wheat noodles, macaroni, or spaghetti

C. VEGETABLES: AT LEAST 2-3 SERVINGS/DAY

1. at least 1 serving/day of the following:
    1 cup cooked or 2 cups raw broccoli*, bok choy*,Brussels
    sprouts, collards*, kale*, mustard greens*, chard, spinach,
    romaine lettuce, carrots, sweet potatoes, winter squash, or
    tomatoes

2. at least 1 serving/day (1 serving equals 1 cup cooked or 2 cups
    raw) of any other vegetable

D. FRUITS: 2-6 SERVINGS/DAY

1. two servings/day of the following:
    3/4 cup berries, 1/4 cantaloupe, 1 orange, 1/2 grapefruit,
    1 lemon or lime, 1/2 papaya, 4-inch x 8-inch watermelon
    slice, or 1/2 cup orange, grapefruit, or calcium-fortified
    orange* juice, or vitamin C-enriched juice

2. additional servings as desired of other fruits:
    1 medium piece fresh fruit
    3/4 cup grapes
    1/2 cup cooked fruit or canned fruit without sugar
    1/4 cup raisins, dates, or dried fruit

E. FATS: 0-4 SERVINGS/DAY

1. one serving equals:
    1 teaspoon vegan margarine or oil
    2 teaspoons mayonnaise or salad dressing
    1 Tablespoon vegan cream cheese, gravy, or cream sauce

F. OMEGA-3 FATS: 2 SERVINGS/DAY

1. one serving equals:
    1 teaspoon flaxseed oil
    3 teaspoons canola or soybean oil
    1 Tablespoon of ground flaxseed
    1/4 cup walnuts

G. STARRED * FOOD ITEMS: 8 OR MORE SERVINGS/DAY; 10 OR MORE SERVINGS/DAY FOR THOSE AGE 51 & OLDER
(Also counts as servings from other groups.)

H. VITAMIN B12 SOURCES: 3 SERVINGS/DAY (4 FOR PREGNANT OR BREASTFEEDING WOMEN)

1. one serving equals:
> 1 Tablespoon Red Star Vegetarian Support Formula
> nutritional yeast
> 1 cup fortified soymilk
> 1 ounce fortified breakfast cereal
> 1-1/2 ounces fortified meat analogs

(Note: if these foods are not eaten regularly, a vitamin B12 supplement of 5-10 micrograms daily or 2,000 micrograms weekly should be used.)

I. ADDITIONAL COMMENTS

1. Additional servings from one or more food groups may be needed to meet energy needs especially for pregnant and breastfeeding women and physically active people.

2. This meal plan is for vegan adults. Meal plans for children can be found on our website: www.vrg.org

3. Items listed under Omega-3 Fats can also count as servings from the fats or protein foods groups, as appropriate.

SAMPLE TWO DAY MENU

	BREAKFAST	LUNCH	DINNER	SNACKS
DAY 1	Peanut butter on toast Fortified orange juice	Bean burritos Carrot and celery sticks Strawberries	Stir-fry with tofu, broccoli, and bok choy Brown rice Ginger snaps	Popcorn sprinkled with nutritional yeast Fortified soymilk
DAY 2	Cold cereal with fortified soymilk Banana	Split pea soup Crackers with almond butter Coleslaw Fresh fruit	Pasta with lentil-spinach-tomato sauce French bread Steamed kale Cantaloupe	Trail mix with soy nuts and raisins Fortified orange juice

Vegetarianism on the Job

A common problem vegetarians encounter is finding something to eat while working. Cafeterias often offer very little food that we can consume besides salads or perhaps a veggie burger. As a result, vegetarians must often bring their own lunch. What happens when you have to attend a business luncheon or travel? The following essays are true stories written by those in the working world who have learned to cope in a meat-eating world. We also include ideas for adults whose job is to raise children.

COMPUTER PROGRAMMER

I work in a building with 300 employees, so our cafeteria has limited selections (almost all of which are not vegan). To save time, I bring my lunch to work every day rather than go out.

I don't like to spend a lot of time during the week preparing lunches, so I try to do any cooking on the weekend. I prepare double or triple batches of vegetarian chili, split pea soup, black bean soup, or lentil soup. Then I freeze individual portions. During the week, I grab one of the items from the freezer and add an apple, a microwaved potato, or half a sandwich. I'll also take leftover spaghetti.

Fortunately, I have a bread machine, which makes preparing delicious whole wheat vegan breads easy. I'll make a loaf on Sunday night and it lasts me throughout the week. Sometimes, I'll also use leftover bagels for lunch that I have put in the freezer.

When I don't take the time to cook in advance, I'll go for convenience foods such as Fantastic Foods Cha-Cha Chili or Five Bean Soup or Cascadian Farms frozen Meals in a Minute. These meals are bags of frozen organic rice and bean mixtures in various flavors such as Indian, Mexican, or Moroccan. You simply add boiling water or heat them up.

REGISTERED DIETITIAN

I've been a nutritionist for over 17 years, but I've been a vegetarian much longer. You would think that vegetarianism would be more prevalent among those who make diet and health their business, but that's not the case.

I'm non-traditional among those in my profession in another way, too. I have a home-based business and make my living as a nutrition consultant. Most of my time is spent in my home office, sitting at my desk, phoning, faxing, and word processing on my computer. My schedule is my own, and that means that I may eat breakfast, lunch, and dinner at times that may be totally out of sync with the outside world.

Others may not see what I eat when I'm working at home, but I keep myself in line. I spend very little time preparing lunch — under 10 minutes — because I'm busy and like to get back to work quickly. Sometimes I heat up leftovers from dinner the night before. Examples may be a slice or two of cheeseless vegetable pizza, a serving of a bean and vegetable casserole, or leftover Chinese take-out. I also like to reheat plain leftover vegetables (especially steamed kale or sweet potatoes) and I eat that with a couple of slices of whole wheat toast and a glass of orange juice. Sometimes I buy fresh carrot juice from the supermarket and mix that with orange juice. It's a delicious blend, and it always seems like a magically healthful "elixir" to me. I don't skimp when it comes to good quality food, and I keep a wide variety on hand.

On the other hand, I've also been known to have a bowl of cereal with soy milk for lunch, especially when I have a favorite kind in the cupboard. I'm a big fan of cereal (dry or hot). Sometimes I even eat it for dessert. Other days, I may cook a potato in the microwave and eat it with ketchup or salsa along with a toasted bagel or English muffin. Another favorite is a sweet potato cooked in the microwave, then topped with a little brown sugar and several "squeezes" of fresh lime juice.

I usually have hummus in my 'fridge, so some days I'll eat that in whole grain pita pockets. Another staple is a bag of baby carrots (the kind that are already peeled), and I'll eat a handful of those, dipped in hummus, along with a peanut butter and banana sandwich. Another common lunch is a big pasta bowl filled with mesclun salad mix. I add about a half cup of garbanzo beans, sliced tomatoes (if they're in season), a few black olives, and some ground black pepper. I top it with flavored vinegar (mango or raspberry vinegar are my favorites). I eat a slice of toast with that, or a piece of fresh fruit.

I care about the quality and presentation of my food. I eat a lot of plain, fresh foods prepared very simply. I take care to make my plate look attractive and even add a garnish now and then — even though it's only me who sees it! I may not spend much time preparing my meals, but I eat very well and enjoy my food immensely.

TEST SATISTICIAN

In the summer I bring cut up fresh tomatoes and make a lettuce and tomato sandwich on whole wheat bread that I bring from home. Otherwise, I eat at the salad bar at work.

During the winter months, I bring hummus, baba ghanouj, or soy cream cheese and tomato sandwiches on whole wheat bread. When I'm rushed I have to resort to the salad bar at work. I may also bring leftover baked potatoes that I microwave. This is typical. On occasion, when I have leftover pasta salads from home, I'll bring that, too.

MUSIC THEORIST AND ADMINISTRATOR

I bring a 1/2 cup of cottage cheese, 2 cups popcorn, and half an apple to work for lunch. I'll also bring a caffeine-free diet soda. (About once a week I go buy a cookie, too!)

WRITER/EDITOR

When I eat lunch, I'm usually at one of three locations: home, an office, or a sporting event. If I'm at home, I may eat small snacks all day (fruit, granola, peanut butter and crackers, etc.) and work right through lunch. If I do sit down to lunch at home, it's frequently comprised of the previous evening's leftovers. I keep whole wheat pitas and tortillas handy at all times and will usually fill a pita or roll a tortilla with leftover grains, vegetables, crumbled tofu or tempeh. Then I just heat and eat. Sometimes, I'll also spread hummus or refried beans on the pita or tortilla and once in a while I'll have a salad or bowl of hot soup on the side.

If I'm at one of the offices where I occasionally work, I might bring some leftovers, a sandwich or a packaged cup of soup or pasta. If not, I'll get a sandwich at a nearby deli or sub shop. A couple of slices of whole wheat bread loaded with vegetables and some hot peppers is a favorite. A few nearby restaurants serve veggie burgers, so I make that an occasional choice. Take-out orders from nearby Thai, Chinese, Italian, Indian, or Mexican eateries fit easily into my eating style. One of my favorite take-out items is a pizza covered with tomato sauce and basil, and dotted with chunks of falafel. Admittedly, you won't find this option at most pizza places, but if you love falafel, you should try creating this work of art at home.

Most of the sporting events I cover are at night, so I'm usually scrambling for dinner options on those evenings. From time to time I do find myself at a matinee hockey game. The home team provides a free meal to the working press two or three hours before game time. Usually this meal consists of the dead critter of the day accompanied by some form of potato, some overly steamed vegetables, a skimpy iceberg lettuce salad, and white rolls. Doesn't exactly make your taste buds dance, does it? If pressed for time, I might suffer through the wilted veggies, the salad, and the potatoes. But more often I'll pack a sandwich and some fruit to eat or try to eat a light lunch at a nearby restaurant. Another option is eating a large, late breakfast and bringing along fruit, granola, crackers, and other light snack items.

EDUCATIONAL TESTING SPECIALIST

I generally have a salad from the salad bar in our cafeteria or two to three hot side dishes such as rice with Brussels sprouts or kale, baked potatoes, or mushrooms. I also eat peanut butter and jelly sandwiches or cheese and onion or lettuce, tomato, and onion sandwiches. Sometimes I have a slice of pizza or a dish of pasta. I also like to bring celery and carrot sticks or an apple for snacks (when I remember to cut up the veggies).

EDUCATION RESEARCHER

I don't like to cook and I don't have a lot of time in the morning to put a bag lunch together. My lunch consists of putting my hand in my freezer and pulling out a Veggie Pocket — they come in several different varieties. I throw a handful of baby carrots in a plastic bag (which I reuse) and take a piece of fruit or two: apples and pears in the fall and winter; peaches and plums in the summer. At lunchtime, I just pop my Veggie Pocket in the microwave for 90 seconds and voila, lunch!

MATHEMATICIAN

I used to have hummus on pita brad and sometimes yogurt or salad. Ocassionally, I'll bring vegetarian cup-of-soups where you can add water and microwave them or add boiling water.

Lately I've been having peanut butter crackers along with a granola bar and juice. I don't typically eat a lot for lunch and I go through different phases.

ACCOUNTANT

My first job after graduating from college was for an accounting firm. At previous jobs, and throughout my life as a student, my vegetarian lifestyle was not a problem to deal with on a daily basis. I either brought my lunch with me or I ate at a place that I knew had vegetarian options available. While working for the accounting firm, however, I was often forced to be more flexible with my eating habits.

Most of the time, I worked at our clients' places of business. Therefore, I was not able to bring my lunch and I often had to go out to eat. Fortunately, I was often able to eat a decent meal. Other times, I needed to be a bit more creative with what I ordered for lunch. On several occasions, I worked at businesses located in small towns that had only one or two eating places. Most of these places were sandwich shops or family restaurants whose only vegetarian options were cheese subs or salads. It was during this time that I began to order what I call a PLT sandwich. This is made of peppers, lettuce, and tomato with the occasional addition of mushrooms when they are available. During one engagement, the only place where we could eat was at this little sandwich shop on the corner across the street. They had a selection of bagel sandwiches, all of which had meat or cheese on them. I ended up asking if they could make me a bagel sandwich with lettuce, tomatoes, and mushrooms. I was amazed at how ordering these sandwiches could cause such a crisis for the people who worked in the restaurant. In the end, however, no one ever denied me my "special orders" and many times I ended up getting a great bargain on the price. One woman who waited on me actually said she might like to try a PLT and that they would even consider adding it to their menu!

My co-workers were often curious about my lifestyle. Initially, a few of them would make sarcastic comments, attempting to make me get angry and defensive about my beliefs. After getting past the "Vegan, what is that?" stage, I believe most of my co-workers have grown to realize that stereotypes are nothing more than blatant generalizations. For just as not every accountant is a boring pocket-protector wearing business person, not every vegetarian looks down upon meat-eating people. As my co-workers learned more about my lifestyle choices, many of them grew to respect me for standing up for what I believe. At the same time, there will always be some people who have absolutely no interest in vegetarianism and I will always respect their freedom to choose their lifestyle. I have learned that the best way for vegetarians to educate others about vegetarianism is to simply live our lives according to our beliefs. There is no good reason to force our opinions on other people. If someone is curious about vegetarianism, they will approach us.

In general, the more often I ate in restaurants, the more I came to realize that there definitely are options available for both vegetarians and vegans. The key to discovering these options is to ask. Although the number of vegetarians is increasing, the majority of people are not vegetarian and menus are merely a reflection of this. However, most restaurants are quite willing to accommodate vegetarians. Regardless of our dietary prefer-ences, we are still paying customers. With creativity and flex-ibility, eating out while on the job is actually quite simple. I have never expected to be able to order tempeh stroganoff or tofu cheesecake, but I have not had a problem ordering a salad with a baked potato, a few fruit cups to make a fruit salad, or a few side dishes of vegetables for a lunch platter. The best way vege-tarians can encourage a restaurant to offer vegetarian dishes on their menu is to continue to request them. Only then can we expect to see more changes.

PARENTS

Lunchtimes are often not sit-down affairs, at least not for me. With two young children stating, "Could I please have more soymilk," "I want (whatever mom is eating," and of course, "I'm through and I need my hands washed (right as mom sits down to eat)" are some of the usual sounds.

So, my criteria for lunch foods are those that are quick to prepare. When my children were younger, I ate a lot of peanut butter. It was quick, it was filling, and it was often what I was fixing for them. We ate PB on bagels (cinnamon raisin bagels are best), PB sandwiches, PB on bananas, and PB on apples. Oh, yes, PB on crackers, too.

Leftovers, are another good, quick lunch. I usually try to have leftovers from dinner as one lunch option. They're often eaten straight out of the refrigerator or they can be reheated in a microwave. My personal favorites are soups, cold vegetables, and pasta.

I often make shakes for the children and may have some myself. These are made by combining half a package of silken soft tofu, some soy milk, a frozen banana or other fruit (strawberries, blueberries, peaches, applesauce, etc.), and maple syrup to taste in the food processor. Leftover frozen dessert (sorbet, Rice Dream, etc.) can also be added. These are good with bread or crackers on the side.

Hummus or some other kind of bean dip is also pretty quick. I eat this in pita bread, with crackers, on a bagel, or with vegetables and apples as dippers.

In the summer, my favorite lunch is a sliced tomato, still warm from the garden, on whole-grain bread or a bagel with spicy mustard. I could live on this!

If breakfast was a hurried affair, I may have a bowl of cold cereal with soy milk and fruit or some oatmeal for lunch. This is always amusing to the children.

My husband is also home during the day. His favorite quick lunches are leftovers, Tofu Pups, and Harvest Burgers. He always takes advantage of the garden in the summer and has veggie sandwiches and salads. And of course, there are the "immediate leftovers" from the children (crusts, rejected special of the day, and anything designated as "yucky."

Nutrient Charts

On the next few pages you will find charts listing good sources of some nutrients for vegans. You can find information about the nutrient content of common food items in the USDA Nutrient Database for Standard Reference. This can be found online at <http://www.nal.usda.gov/fnic/foodcomp>.

The Recommended Dietary Allowances (RDA) are the amounts of nutrients recommended by the Food and Nutrition Board, and are considered adequate for maintenance of good nutrition in healthy persons in the United States.

Please note that in an equal amount of calories, greens such as kale and collards have more calcium, iron, and protein than beef. The key to a healthy vegetarian diet is to eat a wide variety of foods. If you were eating only meat and no vegetables, you would have a hard time meeting your dietary needs.

Vegan Sources of Calcium

Food, serving size	Calcium (milligrams)
Almond butter, 2 TB	86
Bok choy , cooked, 1 cup	167-188
Broccoli, cooked , 1 cup	79
Calcium-fortified orange juice, 1/2 cup	150
Calcium-fortified soy milk, 1 cup	200-300
Collard greens, cooked, 1 cup	357
Figs, dried, 5	137
Kale, cooked, 1 cup	99
Tofu with calcium (read label), 1/2 cup	120-430
Adequate Intake (AI)	1000 (19-50 year olds)
	1200 (> 50 years old)

Vegan Sources of Iron

Food, serving size	Iron (milligrams)
Garbanzo beans, cooked, 1/2 cup	2.4
Kidney beans, cooked, 1/2 cup	2.6
Lentils, cooked, 1/2 cup	3.3
Oatmeal, instant, 1 packet	4.0
Pumpkin seeds, 2 TB	2.5
Soybeans, cooked, 1/2 cup	4.4
Spinach, cooked, 1/2 cup	3.2
Textured vegetable protein, reconstituted, 1/2 cup	2.7
Tofu, firm, 1/2 cup	6.6
Recommended Dietary Allowance (RDA)	14 (vegetarian men and postmenopausal women)
	33 (vegetarian premenopausal women)

Vegan Sources of Zinc

Food, serving size	Zinc (milligrams)
Fortified breakfast cereal, 1 oz	0.7-15
Garbanzo beans, cooked, 1/2 cup	1.3
Peas, cooked, 1/2 cup	1.0
Tahini, 2 TB	1.4
Tofu, firm, 1/2 cup	1.4
Veggie "meats", fortified, 1 oz	1.2-2.3
Wheat germ, 2 TB	2.3
Recommended Dietary Allowance (RDA)	11 (men)
	8 (women)

Note: Some vitamin D can be made by exposure to sunlight but varies according to season and latitude. (See next page for vitamin D food sources.)

Vegan Sources of Vitamin D

Food, serving size	Vitamin D (micrograms)
Fortified breakfast cereal, 1 oz	0.5-1.0
Fortified soy milk, 1 cup	1.0-3.0
Adequate Intake (AI)	5 (19-50 years old)
	10 (51-70 years old)
	15 (>70 years old)

Vegan Sources of Vitamin B-12

Food, serving size	Vitamin B-12 (micrograms)
Fortified breakfast cereal, 1 oz	0.6-6.0
Fortified soy milk, 1 cup	0.0-3.0
Vegetarian Support Formula Nutritional Yeast, 1 TB	4.0
Veggie "meats", fortified, 2.2 ounces	1.2
Recommended Dietary Allowance (RDA)	2.4 (adults)

Vegan Sources of Protein

Food, serving size	Protein (grams)
Bagel, 1	6
Brown rice, cooked, 1 cup	4.9
Garbanzo beans, cooked, 1 cup	14.5
Lentils, cooked, 1 cup	17.9
Peanuts, 1 oz	7.3
Soymilk, 1 cup	6.6
Tofu, 1/2 cup	10
Recommended Dietary Allowance (RDA)	56 (men)
	46 (women)

Spices For Vegetarian Cookery

Types and amounts of spices will vary according to your cooking style. Below are some combinations that have proved to work well. Experiment and enjoy!

ALLSPICE

cakes
breads
baked fruit
beverages

CELERY SEED

soups
coleslaw
potato salad
casseroles
mayonnaise

CHILI POWDER

stews
bean dishes

CINNAMON

oatmeal
breads
teas
apple dishes
cottage cheese
fruit dishes

CUMIN

Mexican dishes
spreads
chili

CURRY POWDER

Indian dishes
rice dishes
tofu
salads

GARLIC POWDER

Italian dishes
beans
salads
vegetables
soups
dips and spreads

MARJORAM

stews
squash
soups

MINT

vegetables
frozen desserts
tea
tabbouli

NUTMEG

apple pie
cheese dishes
desserts

OREGANO

beans
pizza
Mexican dishes
tomato dishes
vegetables
Italian dishes
chili

PAPRIKA

hash browns
vegetables
salads
rice
casseroles
cottage cheese

PARSLEY

salads
bread stuffing
dips
soups
stews

ROSEMARY

dips and spreads
vegetables
soups

TARRAGON

green salads
tomato dishes

THYME

peas and carrots
cheese dishes
onion soup

Egg Replacers (Binders)

Any of the following can be used to replace eggs:
- 1 small banana for 1 egg (great for cakes, pancakes, etc.)
- 2 Tablespoons cornstarch or arrowroot starch for 1 egg
- Ener-G Egg Replacer (or similar product available in health food stores or by mail order)
- 1/4 Cup tofu for 1 egg (blend tofu smooth with the liquid ingredients before they are added to the dry ingredients.)
- 1 Tablespoon ground flaxseed mixed with 3 Tablespoons water for 1 egg

Dairy Substitutes

The following can be used as dairy substitutes in cooking:
- soy milk (add 1 Tablespoon lemon juice or white vinegar to 1 cup soy milk to replace buttermilk in a recipe)
- soy margarine
- soy yogurt (found in health food stores)
- nut milks (blend nuts with water and strain)
- rice milks (blend cooked rice with water)

Meat Substitutes

- tempeh (cultured soybeans with a chewy texture)
- tofu (freezing and then thawing gives tofu a meaty texture; the tofu will turn slightly off white in color)
- wheat gluten or seitan (made from wheat and has the texture of meat; available in health food or Asian stores)
- dried beans
- textured soy protein (1/2 cup dry textured soy protein rehydrated in 1/2 cup boiling water can substitute for 1 cup ground beef)
- Veggie ground round

True or False?

1. Vegetarians have to worry about combining proteins.

2. Milk is the only good source of calcium.

3. Vegans should be aware of good sources of vitamin B12.

4. To be a vegetarian, I have to shop in a health food store and spend a lot of money on groceries.

5. Vegetarian cooking is complicated. I have to change my whole lifestyle to be a vegetarian.

6. Becoming a vegetarian will help me lose weight.

7. Animals in most food advertisements are smiling because they enjoy the good treatment given on farms.

ANSWERS:

1. **FALSE** Vegetarians easily meet their protein needs by eating a varied diet, as long as they consume enough calories to maintain their weight. It is not necessary to plan combinations of foods. A mixture of proteins throughout the day will provide enough essential amino acids. (See "Position of The American Dietetic Association and Dietitians of Canada: Vegetarian Diets," Journal of the American Dietetic Association, June 2003.)

In using the concept of limiting amino acids, many people wrongly assumed this meant there was none of that amino acid in the food. In fact, most foods contain some of all essential amino acids. Exceptions are some fruits and empty calorie or junk foods.

Another important fact is that the body maintains a relatively constant supply of essential amino acids in what is called the amino acid pool. This pool is made up of amino acids from endogenous sources (digestive secretions and desquamated cells) with only a small portion from the diet. The ability of the body to recycle amino acids reassures us that essential amino acids do not need to be eaten in any specific pattern of mealtime or type of food.

Again, the points to remember are to consume a variety of wholesome foods including some protein-rich vegetables and obtain sufficient calories.

2. **FALSE** One cup of whole milk has about 276 milligrams of calcium. One cup of cooked collard greens has 357 milligrams of calcium. Other foods including bok choy, kale, and fortified soymilk and juice also supply calcium.

3. **TRUE** If you do not consume eggs or dairy products, B-12 can easily be obtained from fortified foods such as Red Star's Vegetarian Support Formula brand of nutritional yeast and some fortified breakfast cereals, soymilks, and fake meats. As in any diet, it is helpful to read labels.

4. **FALSE** You can continue to shop at your local supermarket. If you stay away from processed foods and out-of-season fruits and vegetables, a vegetarian diet will probably be much cheaper than a meat-based diet. Compare the price of a salad bar to a steak dinner!

5. **FALSE** Like every other diet, vegetarianism can be complicated or simple. You can continue to eat out and order foods such as eggplant subs, spaghetti, salad bars, baked potatoes, and so on. An added bonus is that you probably will save money by ordering these types of dishes.

6. **FALSE** Again, a vegetarian diet is like any other diet. If you have a normal metabolism, and over consume high-calorie foods such as peanut butter, avocados, nuts, and rich desserts, and do not burn up these excess calories, you will probably gain weight no matter what the sources of these calories.

7. **FALSE** In our observations of animals before slaughter, we have not seen any smiling animals. In order to raise animals for food economically, the animals are kept in crowded conditions. Cows are penned up for several months before slaughter without being allowed to exercise. This prevents the meat from becoming tough. One chicken house could easily contain thousands of chickens, who have very short lives, and do not get to see outside sunlight. Factory farm animals are usually fed antibiotics to prevent illnesses.

Join The Vegetarian Resource Group and Receive Vegetarian Journal

Name _____

Address _____

_____ Zip Code _____

__ Enclosed is $25 for VRG membership and 1-year subscription to Vegetarian Journal.
__ Please charge my (circle one) MasterCard/Visa
   # _____ Expires: ____/____

Send payment and subscription information to The Vegetarian Resource Group, PO Box 1463, Baltimore, MD 21203. Or fax this form to (410) 366-8804. You can charge your membership over the phone by calling (410) 366-8343 Mon.-Fri. 9am to 5pm EST. Additionally, you can join VRG or purchase books on our website at <**www.vrg.org**>. E-mail vrg@vrg.org with any questions.

Simply Vegan — Quick Vegetarian Meals

The immensely popular Simply Vegan, by Debra Wasserman and Reed Mangels, PhD, RD, features over 160 vegan recipes that can be prepared quickly, as well as an extensive nutrition section. The chapters cover topics on protein, fat, calcium, iron, vitamin B12, pregnancy and the vegan diet, and raising vegan kids. Additionally, the book (224 pages) includes sample menus and meal plans. To order, send $18 (including postage) to The Vegetarian Resource Group, PO Box 1463, Baltimore, MD 21203.

To Order More Copies of Meatless Meals for Working People

Send $12 for each book to VRG, PO Box 1463, Baltimore, MD 21203 or call (410) 366-8343; 9am to 5pm Mon.-Fri. EST.

Visit our Website <www.vrg.org>

Index

M-m-m-meatless meals in minutes!

On-the-go vegetarians can have a delicious, all-natural meal in minutes with Fantastic Foods® convenient soups, entrees and side dishes. All our products are shelf-stable so can go where you go!

Convenience doesn't have to mean sacrificing taste. Our perfect blends of premium ingredients and international flavors will please your taste buds while catering to your good health. We add no fillers, artificial ingredients, preservatives or trans fats to our products, and they are very low in saturated fats.

You deserve a great meal. Let Fantastic Foods help you take good care of yourself–even when you're on the run!

FANTASTIC
ALWAYS · NATURAL

fantasticfoods.com

We are proud to sponsor *Meatless Meals for Working People.*